A Month of Sundays

ELEVATING SELF-CARE
TO SOUL-CARE

Davia Williams Stevenson

Copyright © 2024 by Davia Williams Stevenson

ISBN: 978-8-9894995-0-2

Scripture quotations marked NLT are taken from the Holy Bible, New Living Translation, copyright 1996, 2004. Used by permission of Tyndale House Publishers, Inc., Wheaton, Illinois 60189.
All rights reserved.

Neither the publisher nor the author is engaged in rendering professional advice to the reader. The ideas, procedures, and suggestions contained in this book are not intended as a substitute for consulting with your mental health professional. All matters regarding your mental health require professional supervision. Neither the author nor the publisher shall be liable or responsible for any loss or damage allegedly arising from any information or suggestions in this book.

DEDICATION

This book is dedicated you - all of you who desire to live in health and with joy. To those who are willing to look at themselves with honesty, compassion, and grace. To those who seek to care for themselves and their relationships in a mindful and holistic manner. You, who are willing to care for your soul, to appreciate it's beauty, look at the ugly and heal your traumas. Those who desire to grow into a purposed identity and embrace relationship with yourself and your people in truth and in love. Let's together elevate our self-care to soul-care.

CONTENTS

WHAT IS SELF-CARE? ... 1

PHYSICAL ... 6

1 SELF-AWARENESS ... 7
- LIKES AND DISLIKES ... 8
- WHAT IS MY ENERGY LEVEL? ... 11
- WHAT IS MY BODY TELLING ME? ... 12
- BE KIND TO YOURSELF ... 14
- FOR YOUR CONSIDERATION ... 16

2 IDENTITY ... 17
- ROLES AFFECT IDENTITY ... 21
- SELF-PERCEPTION ... 24
- PERSPECTIVE AFFECTS IDENTITY ... 25
- IDENTITY EVOLUTION ... 29
- NURTURING THE SIGNIFICANT ... 32
- FOR YOUR CONSIDERATION ... 35

3 SABBATH ... 37
- BRIEF MOMENTS OF REST ... 38
- LONGER RESPITES ... 40
- FOR YOUR CONSIDERATION ... 42

4 BOUNDARIES ... 43
- TYPES OF BOUNDARIES ... 47
- DEALBREAKERS AND TRICKY BOUNDARIES ... 50
- ENFORCING BOUNDARIES ... 55
- DECIDING WHICH BOUNDARIES APPLY ... 58
- FOR YOUR CONSIDERATION ... 59

MENTAL ... 61

5 PERFECTIONISM AND FEAR ... 62

WAYS WE STRIVE	65
BETTER THAN PERFECT	68
SETTING THE STANDARD	70
FOR YOUR CONSIDERATION	72

6 DREAMS & ASPIRATIONS ... 73

MAKING ROOM FOR DREAMS	75
DREAM DRIVERS	79
BOX FREE	82
SKY'S THE LIMIT	84
FOR YOUR CONSIDERATION	86

7 PRIORITIES ... 87

PUT YOURSELF ON THE LIST	88
BREAKS IN THE DAY	92
INTENTIONAL BODY MOVES	95
IMPORTANCE OF REST	97
FOR YOUR CONSIDERATION	100

8 PERSEVERANCE ... 101

SHADES OF PERSISTENCE	103
CONSCIOUS	104
REFLEXIVE	105
PERSEVERANCE AND SELF-CARE	107
FOR YOUR CONSIDERATION	109

EMOTIONAL ... 110

9 GRIEF AND LOSS ... 111

UNGRIEVED LOSSES AFFECT RELATIONSHIPS	115
ANNIVERSARIES, GUILT, AND GROWTH	117
DEALING WITH GRIEF AND LOSS	121
FOR YOUR CONSIDERATION	125

10 HAPPINESS AND JOY 126

- HAPPINESS SNARE 128
- LOOKING FOR HEAVEN 129
- FLEETING HAPPINESS 130
- FOR YOUR CONSIDERATION 132

RELATIONAL 133

11 FRIENDSHIP 134

- BIRDS OF A FEATHER 135
- FRIEND-VIEW MIRROR 137
- FRIENDS ENCOURAGE 139
- REFLECTIONS OF OURSELVES 140
- LOST OR BROKEN 142
- INTIMATE FRIENDS 144
- REASON, SEASON, LIFETIME 146
- FOR YOUR CONSIDERATION 147

12 CONFLICT 149

- CONFLICT EFFECTS 151
- PLAN TO SUCCEED 153
- USE THE LADDER 155
- MIND READING 157
- LANGUAGE BARRIERS 159
- BEING FULLY PRESENT 162
- CULTURAL AWARENESS 164
- CURIOSITY OR JUDGMENT? 165
- FLATTEN THE CONFLICT CURVE 167
- FOR YOUR CONSIDERATION 171

13 FORGIVENESS 172

- BRING YOUR MIND TO EMOTIONS 175
- PURSUING FREEDOM 176
- DECIDING TO FORGIVE 179
- TREASURE IN THE TEMPEST 183
- CHOOSING THE OUTCOME 184
- FOR YOUR CONSIDERATION 185

SPIRITUAL 186

14 INSPIRATION 187

- CAPTURING INSPIRATION 190
- THIS PRESENT STILLNESS 191
- WHERE INSPIRATION LIVES 194
- FOR YOUR CONSIDERATION 196

15 GRATITUDE 197

- FOCUS RETUNING 199
- THANKFULNESS VS. GRATITUDE 201
- SIGNIFICANT SOURCES 202
- ACKNOWLEDGING THE GOOD 205
- FOR YOUR CONSIDERATION 207

16 RECEIVING INPUT 208

- EVALUATING RESOURCES 209
- SPIRITUAL SOURCES 211
- OPPOSING INPUT 213
- RECEPTIVITY 214
- INTERNAL INPUT 217
- FOR YOUR CONSIDERATION 219

17 MOVING THROUGH **220**
- MANAGING THE COST 223
- THOUGHTS AS THINGS 225
- BELIEF OR TRUTH 227
- FINISHING STRONG... 231
- FOR YOUR CONSIDERATION 234
- APPENDIX 235

A Month of Sundays

What is Self-care?

Self-care Sunday is a hot topic in the social media world right now, and it seems largely--but certainly not limited to—the purview of women. The intention is to be thoughtful about recovering from the previous week and preparing yourself for the week ahead. This is good, essential even, but not sufficient. I notice a deeper desire for individuals to take back personal sovereignty over areas of their day-to-day lives. A pursuit to excel in all areas personal and professional while maintaining an enviable body and pristine environment; a mandate to boss-up, so to speak.

It isn't healthy to run and run and run without respite. This has also birthed conversations about wanting "a soft life." It's an interesting tension. How does one reconcile these seemingly opposing messages? Do you have to choose, or is there a way to have both? Rather than choosing one or the other, let's wrestle with the truth in the tension between the two. Amid this tension is you, a real person living a real life.

My journey as a daughter, sister, wife, mother, grandmother, and clinician informs what I've learned about caring for the self at all levels. I can't perform good mental, emotional, relational, or productive work on a depleted foundation.

Life is full of surprises; there will always be events outside of your control. How you manage to care for yourself through these circumstances and various life stages profoundly impact how you navigate life. This book isn't about spa-day massages, manicures, and vacations—which are all wonderful in their own way. Do these things if you can. However, foundational care, caring for your soul, is the bedrock upon which all other facets of self-care build.

The ability to fulfill roles and weather personal storms is deeply connected to physical self-care. Aside from your physical being, we'll explore four other important levels of care: mental, relational, emotional, and spiritual. By discussing these you'll begin seeing that what affects one part affects all parts. Examples in each chapter will help you understand how you may be impacted. Addressing concerns as they arise will promote more harmony with the self.

For example, if you're concerned about a situation—which occurs in the mental realm—you may not be eating or sleeping well. This, in turn, affects your physical health. Without enough rest or drinking enough water, you may feel lethargic or seem depressed. This potentially results in a distorted perspective or less productive day. In this book, I present options for better solutions. You'll become more aware of how different parts affect one another, and specifically how they affect you.

Our choices and responses can bring us much joy and healing. Gaining self-knowledge helps you reach a deeper understanding of who you are. It assists you in recognizing potential, clarifies where boundaries need to be set, and keeps you tuned in to how you operate in the world.

Elevated self-care allows you to ask deeper questions and drill into thought and behavioral patterns. It gives you the freedom to provide room to breathe, feel, learn, fail, and succeed—to approach your life and relationships with authenticity and presence of mind. The processes covered in *A Month of Sundays* are designed to increase your understanding of what you need and why you need it. It helps you to seek healthy ways to pursue what matters most to you.

This level of care means leaning into emotional work, which allows you the freedom to stop outsourcing your emotions to those things that have unintended consequences. Unprocessed emotions can leave you feeling depleted and unavailable to yourself and others. By simply acknowledging inner wounds, they can begin to heal. When negative patterns stop taking up residence, you feel lighter, happier, and more energized. As you proceed through ever-expanding levels of self-awareness, you see yourself more clearly, recognize your needs, and can more easily find rest and maintain your inner peace.

I'll share common human experiences (many of them my own) with principles and wisdom that has worked for me and many others. For Your **Consideration** questions at the end of each chapter are provided to promote deep thinking, inner healing, and outer well-being. They provide a way for you to interact with the concepts quickly and easily. As you go through *A Month of Sundays,* you may find journaling and revisiting the chapter(s) that speak to you helpful. I encourage you to record your new insights or fresh understandings and notice how they change over time.

My sincere hope is that this becomes your go-to resource that you revisit to refresh specific areas of concern. And that you develop a deeper, more meaningful lifestyle of self-care, a centered soul, and potentially a softer life.

PHYSICAL

1 Self-Awareness

Getting the most out of this book requires a desire to grow in self-awareness. Your awareness builds from being able to observe your thoughts, behaviors and interactions, and the responses you get from others. In a nutshell, self-awareness is knowing who you are, accepting yourself, and making room for your idiosyncrasies in daily experience. Elevated self-care builds upon this foundation.

It takes time to get to know this person that you are, and it's important to remember that it's a lifelong process. What we'll focus on in this brief chapter is how self-awareness is necessary for self-care. As we pay attention to the process, it evolves with us. The topic of self-awareness will resurface many times in the upcoming chapters. For now, we'll touch on some key topics that will help you begin paying attention to how it figures in your tailored self-care.

Likes and Dislikes

Knowing what you like and don't like is a good place to start. You may choose to keep a list or journal about this. Upon doing so, you can start digging into the why behind your preferences. You may dislike something because you had one bad experience. You may like something because of a good experience, or because it was the favorite of someone you cared about, thus an attachment to a memory or relationship. You could potentially decide you really do like something on the second or third try. It's possible that more information changes your perspective.

You may observe that you're not a morning person. Why aren't you? Do you stay up too late, or is there another reason? If you find it impossible to rise in the early hours, taking a job that requires you to get up early may be a struggle. You may find that you're chronically late. Not only will this cause tension at work between you and your boss but also coworkers. At some point, it will likely affect how you feel about the job and yourself. However, getting a job with later hours to accommodate your internal clock shows a level of awareness. Instead of struggling, you now set yourself up for success.

As we mature, we will have many experiences that will inform who we are. Our upbringing is a powerful factor. For example, if you come from a very utilitarian background, where productivity or task completion is highly valued, you may not have been exposed to the arts. But upon exposure to experiences like theater, painting, dance, or architectural design, you may now see things through a new artistic lens. If you enjoy creating things, this may be a new level of awareness for you to pursue. Now you'll notice beauty wherever you go, and you may search for ways to incorporate it into your self-care. When you feel depleted, you may have expanded avenues to replenish yourself. You may find painting, drawing, or sculpting nurtures your soul in a way that being task driven does not. Certainly, the reverse holds true. Completing a task and knocking something off your list may give you rest and peace. Self-awareness is self-discovery.

At every age, I become more self-aware. I learn different things and choose to act out of different strengths. I have less fear about trying something new. Self-awareness can inform whether I should accept or work on different weaknesses.

An example is how I've always approached my schoolwork. Even in grad school, I told myself I'd have a different system, that I would work on papers a little at a time. I implemented some things and maintained a framework. But pretty much every paper, whether three pages or twenty, I wrote overnight or all in one sitting. I often found myself last-minute scrambling. During that time, my focus was laser sharp. My frazzled efforts consistently resulted in a high grade, so why change it?

I acknowledge that my subconscious habit has been to create an emergency because it forced me to be more efficient. I am now aware this is also a likely function of my ADHD. My self-awareness revealed that I function at a higher level in an emergency; I see how this "emergency state" carries over into other areas. But I ask myself, at sixty years of age, is that something I'm going to spend a lot of time changing? I don't think so. The difference being this process has now moved from a subconscious coping habit to a conscious part of my process (and my charm!). It no longer produces the kind of stress and self-accusation it used to.

Here's another example. A certain young man is aware that he doesn't like to eat many different foods but decides to go on a mission trip. In a culture where sharing food represents acceptance and fosters fellowship, he realized that this would require him to eat unfamiliar foods in a foreign country. With the understanding that the mission was of greater importance to him than his personal preferences, he willingly made changes for something of higher value. Understanding how he was limited freed him to expand his view.

Before the mission trip, he was not motivated to change his behavior. His self-awareness allowed him to prepare for this eventuality and connect in meaningful ways with people in their culture.

This experience changed his whole approach to food, to travel and to fellowship. He's more open and has an expanded repertoire of what he enjoys. It all started with what would seem a simple acknowledgment of likes and dislikes, values, and choices.

What is My Energy Level?

Another area of self-awareness is regarding the level of energy you have on any given day. I often counsel folks, "Don't go in debt against yourself." You know how you feel when you're firing on all cylinders, and you know when you're depleted. If you try to function at a level you don't have the gas for – trying to operate at a ninety when you feel like a fifty—you're going into debt against yourself. That debt is going to be called in at some point. It may show up as an emotional breakdown, a health crisis, or in the quality of what you produce, whatever that may be.

Constantly living out of deficit carries high cost. If you're only at 20 percent, live out of your twenty. That's an excellent day. You'll have used 100 percent of the resources you had for that day.

Communicating at a better level is freeing and validating and increases self-awareness. Whenever you know you don't have much to give yourself, and by extension not much to give somebody else, you can express that. All it requires is the ability to self-assess compassionately and honestly. Lord willing, His mercies are new every morning. Tomorrow could be a better day.

What is My Body Telling Me?

Circumstances, conversations, the people you hang out with, and the places you go have an effect on your body. Do they make you feel good? Depleted? Exhilarated? Energized? Tingly or jumpy? Developing an awareness of bodily sensations provides important information.

Pause for a moment to listen to how you feel

in your body, where you are, who you're with. Start connecting dots. My body feels ___ when I'm at this location. I always feel ___ when I spend time with this person. I feel ___ after eating certain types of foods. You're bringing your awareness to the present moment and noticing how you're affected. Then you can determine how to interpret a moment or experience and whether to continue or make changes.

Sometimes when I'm working on something, I'll hit a level of frustration. That's when I practice the pause and ask myself some questions. What am I feeling right now? Do I want to continue or take a break? Do I want to complete this, or set it aside for another day? Sometimes I'll change the scenery. If I'm inside, I might go outside for a while. Sit, take a walk, or grab a drink of water. Or, like I chose to do one day, I can tune in to YouTube and learn a new skill—like line dancing. It was fun, I learned something new, and I felt good about myself.

A pause can be restful, restorative, or constructive. It's your time. Your pause. It's up to you how long that pause needs to be. It can be a few seconds, a few hours, or a few days. What does your body tell you about your needs? Maybe it's a few moments of deep breathing or a nap. Maybe it's going to a park to appreciate nature or being near a body of water. It could be as simple as getting a hug or processing with another person or as complex as leaving a relationship. Over the years, clients who made the difficult choice to leave a toxic relationship often report that they knew in their body before it became conscious in their minds. Conversely, many have shared that they knew a relationship was safe because of how they felt in their body. Begin to listen to your body—it has a lot to tell you.

Be Kind to Yourself

As you grow in self-awareness you must learn to be kind and consider the words you say to yourself. Would you say those same words to somebody else? When we call ourselves names, minimize our value, or engage in negative self-talk, it can too quickly become a habit. Are your words setting the stage for a joyful you or a diminished you?

I've learned to catch myself. There was a time I wasn't aware of how consistently I repeated negative narratives until one day my husband called me out on it. I took that lesson into my practice. If clients repeated certain negatives, I'd ask, "Do you know that you say *can't* all the time?" or "I'm sorry," or "I should?"

"Should" is at the top of the list as a self-shaming word. You make decisions based on the resources you have in the moment. If you live another moment, you get to make a better choice. Consider using life-affirming words and being kind to yourself. Make note of your words.

The words you repeat are part of your "stuck cycle." Almost everyone has a few repeat phrases. I challenge you to count yourself; keep a notepad and add a hashmark each time you catch yourself. This exercise can be jarring, but once you see it, you can choose gentler words.

We all share the same core longings to be loved, to belong, have purpose and significance, and to feel safe and secure. Because of your upbringing and personality development, usually one or two of those places are more vulnerable. Those vulnerabilities will drive almost everything you do.

For instance, if your core longing is for security, insecurity may be reflected in how you handle money. If you're close-handed with any resources, it's possible you're trying to make sure you have enough of what you need.

We don't always know the unmet core longings are driving us. But self-awareness and sometimes therapy can reveal those tendencies. Throughout the book, I'll provide tools that can help you grow in self-awareness. We'll touch on this very important topic many more times in future chapters.

For Your Consideration

1. Pause. Observe yourself. What are you thinking? Can you describe what you're feeling?
2. Slowing down is critical to understanding what you feel in your body. What do you sense? Are you holding tension, anxiety, fatigue?
3. Of these core longings, love, belonging, security, purpose, and significance, do you have a sense of your core vulnerability? What need may be unmet? How is this driving your life?

2 Identity

You begin the journey of learning who you are as soon as you recognize that you're different and separate from those around you. Your identity is who you understand yourself to be. Your ability to express that understanding grows in tandem with the recognition that you have agency over your own thoughts and actions. You may wonder how your identity affects your self-care. I see it as part of identity formation.

You were born an individual. How does that individual show up in life? The things we can't change about ourselves like skin color and genetic history, affect our perception of ourselves. How we identify with our ethnic heritage is also important and may carry wounding and/or displacement, as in the case of African Americans, First Nations, or

Holocaust survivors, to name a few. Names and titles also affect how you see yourself, as well your understanding of your position in relation to others. Choosing your own title is self-care.

If I ask, "Who are you?" Most people respond with what they do. When identifying yourself by your roles, are you elevating them to such a level that you don't see yourself? How do you maintain and care for yourself as you enact those roles? What does that person need to be free to love others? Free to grow in their understanding of personal identity? Knowing who you are is how you know what you need.

Using biblical imagery, I recall the story about Jesus asleep in the boat while a storm raged all around, rocking the security of his disciples. Jesus wasn't disturbed. He was at peace. He understood who he was, whose he was, and his power in that identity. The person who understands they are a child of the king behaves very differently from the one who sees themselves as the child of a pauper.

When you understand who you are, you're able to assess what you need to care for yourself. How you refer to yourself and what you think of yourself matters. It matters individually, it matters culturally, and it matters socially. Do you prefer divorcée or newly single? Do you prefer business owner, entrepreneur, or self-employed? What title makes you feel best about yourself?

It also makes a difference how people refer to you, keeping in mind that you have a level of control over what you let in. You can set a boundary about what you will answer to. What you answer to is linked to how much you value and respect yourself. This directly affects the way you care for yourself — even whether you care for yourself.

Whether ones appreciate your value or not does not diminish your true value in any way. Because outside influences can affect how you perceive yourself and by extension, your personal value, it's important to be watchful regarding what you believe about yourself.

Part of my own personality development was believing that my value was tied to making everybody else happy — putting them first. I wanted to ensure that people were pleased with me. As a result, everybody knew Davia, the charmed Davia, who survived cancer in a single bound! Who still graduated from high school with honors! This is my persona — the public me that I allowed others to see. I received validation by being known and indispensable.

Growing up in a house with my parent's contentious marriage, I learned to be my little sister's protector. As I've grown in self-awareness, I'm now able to see the beginnings of my protector/caregiving/people-pleasing persona.

Many folks would say, "She's just blessed. It's going to work out for Davia because she's Davia. She lives a charmed life. Of course, she married the super successful guy and lives in the gorgeous house and goes to the wonderful places."

Though I'm greatly blessed, I am not "charmed." That dismisses my pain, my trials, and my development, and my hard work. Each stage of my life has not been without many struggles. I own my development: who I am, my shadow side, my strengths, and my trauma. Like most, I had to fight to get this far. How I showed up for myself during a time when I thought I was going to die has forever impacted how I do life. I'm blessed because the Heavenly Father chose to bless me; that isn't something any of us can earn.

If I tell you I'm a two-time cancer survivor, you still don't know me, but you know that experience was part of my development. Cancer does not define me. However, it deeply affects how I take care of myself even now, decades later. It is worth taking a moment to consider what outside influences and experiences are currently affecting your perception of your value. How does this influence your self-care?

Roles Affect Identity

We're prone to thinking that the roles we fulfill are our identity. While they're good information, like boundaries, they feed your understanding of where you end, and others begin. Your understanding of self, shifts, changes, and develops over the course of your lifetime. And it requires a more nuanced understanding to remember that your roles are only part of who you are.

Sometimes we take on roles that cause a major identity shift. Parenting is a perfect example. Many parents have shoved all their personal hopes, dreams, and plans to the side in order to care for their children. Years later, when their family grows up and moves on with their lives, these parents realize their identity became tied to their children. Without the need to constantly care for them, their sense of self seems lost. Empty nesters understand this all too well.

As I developed in my various roles, (wife, mother, sister) the way I embodied them was largely to deny myself. Selflessness is tied to our sense of duty to those around us. I've often said, we (women, in particular) are good at taking care of people, but don't forget *you, too,* are a people!

I didn't always make myself a "people" in ways that nurtured my body, mind, or soul. There were inclinations, however. One of my traditions when I took the boys school shopping was to get myself a little something too. It was a little reminder that I'm a person that also had needs. In those early days, I didn't really know the full extent of those needs, nor did I have a framework for the importance of what is now called self-care.

As parents, we make sure our little ones are fed well, get proper rest, and teach them appropriate social skills for functioning in society. We entertain them, educate them, and repeat important lessons we want etched in their minds. We value them by spending time with them, speaking kindly and patiently, and investing in every level of their enrichment and development. We highlight and encourage their strengths and teach them to channel those in healthy ways. Are we caring for our adult selves in the same way?

Early on if someone had asked me, "Who are you?" I would have answered, "I'm a wife. I'm a mother" But "wife" and "mother" are not my identity, but they are my roles, albeit my primary roles. Now I have a clearer understanding of who I am.

"I'm Davia. I'm married to my husband. I have two sons. I do clinical work, coaching, and podcasts. I've written a book." I'm not only an author, or clinician any more than I am cancer.

Additionally, my faith also informs my understanding and beliefs about identity. I believe our greatest, core identity is shaped by what God says about us. You are created on purpose for a purpose. Because of my Christian faith, I believe we are made for worship. If I say that my identity is in Christ—it means my practice of self-care will include fortifying myself spiritually. It also impacts my belief regarding how I carry out my roles and how I move in my community. My faith impacts my understanding of my responsibilities. As my identity continues to evolve, the options for how I execute said roles increase. I see myself as my own unit who needs to show up for myself—even as I show up for others.

We all struggle with trying to understand who we are, our relationship to ourselves, to others, and to our community and the world at large. How you understand yourself and your place in the world is cumulative and shifts a bit over time. As society provides more options, identity development is even more complex. The expanded understanding of identity development and the embodiment of our significant roles isn't either/or, but both/and. It provides the foundation for the full expression of yourself in the fulfillment of your roles without losing yourself to those very roles.

Self-Perception

Each of us is born naked and alone—imbued with purpose from The Creator. Over time, we develop tendencies and discover preferences. These elements (among others) are expressions of personality which, according to many experts, are solidly established in the latter stage of early childhood. My mother wrote her observations in my toddler book; that I was bright, and curious. She wrote further that I enjoyed attention, liked words, was friendly toward most people and was a bit rebellious. At that time, as a daughter and little sister, I had no roles and no responsibilities. But those core traits absolutely reflect who I am to this day.

Over time, I took on roles like wife and mother. My identity transcends those roles. That means I would still be the person my mother saw, even if I never married or had children. My identity is separate though intertwined with my roles. I am yet and still the individual born decades ago.

We aren't born knowing ourselves. An artist, athlete, or musician isn't born with the knowledge of their talents. Over time, by pursuing their interests and curiosities, those talents are discovered like treasures. Each person chooses if they'll develop those gifts and talents and to what degree. Exposure to new ideas, experiences, and roles help reveal interests and capabilities. Discovery is self-care. Make time to find or pursue those hidden giftings. You can then decide if, how, or when they will enrich your life.

Perspective Affects Identity

The illustration on the next page is based on the Johari Window graphic. Each section represents your identity with regard to your self-awareness.

Each of us regularly operates in these spaces. At the top left corner, our public self is what we understand about ourselves and what we allow to be public. The indefinite self is what you don't see about yourself but is seen by others. It's a blind area for you and an area of potential growth or understanding if you're able to receive input from others.

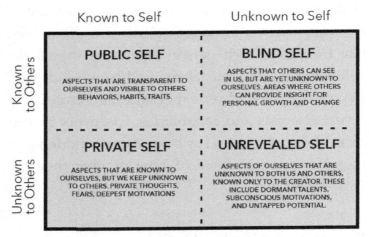

Davia Williams-Stevenson, 2024 - Permission to use for therapy purposes
Adapted from The Johari Window Model (Joseph Luft and Harry Ingham)

When you gain understanding about who you are, it influences self-care.

In the lower left half are those things that you know about yourself, but choose to keep private, out of the public eye. This segment holds great potential for exploration and self-discovery. Here is where you question your why. Why am I keeping this private? Is it because I freely choose to be private with it, or because it's a secret? Is it something painful? Is it a shame? Is it fear? By evaluating your why, you can decide if you'd like supportive input from others or from God.

Finally, the yet to be revealed or disclosed quadrant contains mysteries; that which is not yet known to us or anyone else. From my spiritual paradigm, that's where God works. This is why you're able to continue discovering more about yourself and learning about abilities, gifts, and interests you didn't know you had.

These boxes are fluid. You can move things from private to public, you can learn about your blind areas from others, you can uncover new things and expand your understanding of self. And as you do, they will likely change how you care for yourself. The bottom line is, as you understand who you are within these boxes and what can flow, then you can know what you need.

For instance, when I'm in a depressed or anxious mood, it isn't the time to make big decisions or have important discussions. I sit still and listen to music or ocean sounds. Sometimes hearing the same song over and over calms me. Sometimes it's the lyrics or the chords or the message. In a gospel song called "Let Go," it was the concept that hooked me. I learned to "let go" of how the story ends, to be present with God rather than project or try to influence the outcome. God revealed how I could do that. It was discovery, music, feeding my spirit and mind. All self-care.

When my husband is depressed, he moves his body; he chooses to be active rather than sit still. While he's engaged in physical activity, he's thinking and processing. What works for Eric doesn't work for me, nor does mine work for him. We each know what we need. As you understand yourself, you will more consistently choose what works for you.

We all have blind areas—even the person who sees yours so clearly. It's part of our construction. If you were a driver traveling with someone, they would tell you if you were too close to the car traveling next to you on the freeway. A car has blind spots, and to mitigate them, they're built with mirrors. We are not cars, and it requires a level of humility and trust to allow someone to speak into our life and hear what they have to say. By accepting the input of a trusted person, you can improve vision and perspective you otherwise can't gain unaided. Keep in mind, this is an ongoing process; other blind areas will replace them. Just as you never get rid of the mirrors on a car, hold on to those trustworthy people willing to speak honestly to you.

"Using our illustration on page 25, let's explore an example of a woman who is a wife and mother. What's public is her role. What is clear to others but not known to her, is that she is an overprotective mother.

What is privately known to her is that she's in an abusive marriage. She keeps this to herself because she's afraid and/or ashamed. What has yet to be revealed to her is how to change her circumstances. If she moved information about her abusive marriage to what is public, folks who care about her could shed light on her blind spot and speak to her about options for changing her situation. What might be revealed is her strength to address this situation through counseling, standing up for herself, or creating a strategy to leave. In that instance, she gains more knowledge about her blind area, which allows her to change the way she cares about herself.

Identity Evolution

It used to be common to hear about identity crisis. Even now, the words carry a negative connotation, as though you fell apart. I view it as something wonderful. Crises are like brass cymbals in a musical crescendo. It's a big "WAKE UP!" moment. In a marching band, we want the excitement of cymbals but on their own, we describe cymbals as clashing.

As in most things, the context matters. I don't consider crisis a bad thing. Webster offers alternate definitions: a crisis can be a turning point (for better or worse); an emotionally significant event or a decisive moment. Many of us will have multiple crises of identity at different stages of our lives. Not all will be painful or dramatic. Some will be enlightening, energizing, or revelatory.

In a simpler time, identity formation was very tied to roles, and it seemed easier to know how and where you fit. As our world becomes more global, information more accessible, and choices continue to increase, it might feel more difficult for people to know where they fit in the world and sometimes even in their own heads.

A client I worked with years ago went through a type of identity crisis when her art career began stalling out. On the heels of that, her husband announced his plans to annul their marriage. One of the stipulations of their agreement was that she could no longer use his last name. Initially she was upset, having invested many years incorporating the name into her brand. While venting to a sympathetic boss, his perspective caught her off-guard.

"Wait. You get to *reinvent* yourself?"

The question changed the paradigm. She had

the opportunity to write a new chapter and leave her old stories behind. She chose a name that reflected her joy and passion, then legally changed it.

"It transformed my life. Now, people hear my name, and they smile. It is never mispronounced, and it's memorable. There were over six hundred people with my former name. Now there's only one. And because of that, I'm much more mindful of how I move in the world. Because the name makes people smile, I wanted to embody a certain level of joy and encouragement. It helped me pay attention to what I think, how I act, and the words I say. I'm more mindful about how I interact with people because they're probably going to remember the name and I'm easy to find."

This new perspective on her crisis radically changed everything. This ending became a new beginning in which she found a rewarding career and moved on to a healthier, more nurturing relationship with herself and eventually a new partner. How you see yourself, name yourself, matters.

What are you searching for? What helps you understand who you are? Very few people understand all things about themselves, or all their interactions with other people. If you're working to figure out who you are and where you fit in this world, welcome to humanity!

Nurturing the Significant

I worked with a young lady on and off over many years. In our first interaction, she carried a lot of false bravado. At school, she was often getting into fights and self-described as a "ghetto white girl."

Shortly after we met, her boyfriend, who was her first love, was shot and killed. At school, she was volatile, and her grades began falling. In addition to that, her family was going through a public airing of private struggles which caused further anguish and embarrassment. My focus was on reigning in her behavior, though not at the expense of her dignity.

I understood that her behavior was the end of the line—the evidence of grief, loss, humiliation, and identity questions. Because of her special circumstances, I weighed in very strongly against certain school policies that, if enforced, would cause further—possibly irreparable—damage. Despite her tough talk, our young lady was in a fragile state.

Thankfully, the powers that be were convinced to shift their focus toward helping her graduate. My attention centered on those characteristics that were exhibited even during her extreme behaviors. I chose to point out her core values in the hopes of channeling them toward more positive expressions.

"You have a very strong sense of justice," I said.

"What do you mean?"

"Right and wrong matters to you. That's a sense of justice. We don't want to get rid of that," I said. "You are fiercely loyal to the people you love. And you will go to bat to make sure they are fair and treated fairly. You value respect and loyalty. We don't want you to lose that either."

It was important to show her I saw something different in her. I didn't see her as the school staff did. I was looking at her heart and found those character traits that made her different from others, the values that she had prioritized. It was also clear that she struggled with how to impose order on a traumatic life that felt chaotic. She had created many self-protective layers which would be dealt with over time. Initially, she couldn't see this.

As I shared my insights with her, she saw and understood a greater purpose for herself and began modifying certain behaviors. She graduated, found meaningful employment, and began developing her own business. Because of her fierce loyalty and deep love. She is still the same person at the core: still loyal, still a strong sense of justice, still loves deeply. But she chooses whether to engage in self-protective behaviors.

Her personality traits didn't change. She was willing to fight for what she believed in, which wasn't bad. But those beliefs needed a positive outlet. As her identity continued to develop, she was able to reframe them so she could see her positive characteristics. By giving them a name, she was able to redirect that energy.

She's still figuring out who she is and how she fits in the world. She is fundamentally the same young woman—still fiercely loyal and still has a need to fight. Because I know her story, I understand her sense of justice and why she defends people she feels were wronged. Now she can determine if her behavior and loyalties fit with where she's going. And if not, she can develop a plan that helps her remain true to herself while moving forward.

Clarifying your identity is like tightening focus on a camera. The view through the lens becomes sharpened as *long as you embrace the various and evolving aspects of yourself.*

Understand that we're all special but

we're not really that unique. The human experience is largely everybody's human experience. The things we struggle with tend to be the things that all people struggle with. It's normal to struggle while clarifying our identity. Nearly everyone goes through this several times throughout life.

In your struggle for clarity, your cultural or societal context informs who you are. You are tuned in to social cues. You send signals out and get signals back. The way you take care of yourself is by letting yourself be the things that you are. Love yourself enough to accept who you are and where you are. But also be willing to love yourself enough to invest and change if that's what you need to do.

For Your Consideration

1. While paying attention to your use of roles-focused language or qualities-focused language, how would you describe yourself?
2. Currently, what are your most important roles? Regarding your personality, what aspects do you struggle with? What feelings are difficult for you to address?

3. On a piece of paper, write out your answers for the questions above. Make your thoughts

things. Acknowledge who you are at this moment. What does this person need?

3 Sabbath

When you hear the word sabbath, what comes to mind? For many it could mean the biblical seventh day of rest. For certain religious societies, Sunday is a sabbath day to cease from work, pour into yourself spiritually, and spend time with family. And while that is largely accurate, for the purposes of this book we'll focus more on what I call "the principle of sabbath," a secondary definition meaning a time of restoration.

What this principle shares with the original sabbath is the practice of pulling away from all daily cares and responsibilities as a means to restore and refresh. Rest is basic foundational self-care, along with drinking water, moving your body, and breathing deeply.

I first heard about the principle of the sabbath

when the late Marva Dawn spoke as a guest at the congregation I attended. In her book, *Keeping the Sabbath Wholly,* what stood out to me was the importance of pulling away from the larger world. To reap the rewards of this principle, you must make a time of rest regular and cyclical.

In our demanding and overly busy society, not everybody can take a whole day or a half-day. Even if they can, it may not be weekly. Maybe you're in a stage of life that doesn't permit a full day. Sometimes with a house full of children, a job, a spouse or partner, caring for parents, and a full plate of commitments, taking time to rest may seem impossible. For this reason, I've expanded the sabbath concept to include shorter moments of rest.

Brief Moments of Rest

First, let's define the parameters of the sabbath principle: It must be cyclical and regular. If you expand your perspective of sabbath, you can string moments together as you go through your day, each day. This can be done no matter how chaotic or how busy or demanding your life is.

We all have cyclical and regular habits that we engage. To which activities from the following

list can you attach moments of rest?
- Waking up
- Going to bed
- Brushing your teeth
- Eating a meal
- Driving somewhere
- Using the bathroom

Then ask yourself how you might tie thirty seconds—a minute, or two minutes—to one of them. Whatever you choose may be as simple as making sure you're breathing deeply. Take an extra thirty seconds while driving, brushing your teeth, or waiting for an appointment to breathe in through your nose the deepest breath you can comfortably hold for a count of four. Release slowly through your lips to a count of four. Pause for a count of four. Breathe in deeply to a count of four, hold four beats, exhale four beats. Repeat two more times. While you breathe in this way, imagine your body becoming calm. Peace washes over you.

Whatever refreshes you, make it regular and cyclical. Maybe it's drinking water on every visit to the bathroom; you can get four ounces of water down in about six gulps. While you're driving somewhere, listen to a message that lifts you up or revives your spirit. In the morning, before getting out of bed, or getting ready for bed, do some stretches. Restful moments can be created through journaling, reading a devotion each day, or making time for meaningful prayer.

Those extra moments are for your benefit only. Through this process of mini sabbaths, you begin carving out a little time, little respites for yourself. If or when you're able to take longer moments, do that which fills and revives you.

Longer Respites

It's important to point out what a sabbath does not include. Since this is time meant for refreshing, anything that does not accomplish that goal is off the list. For me personally, a sabbath is not for paying bills or running errands. There are no pressing appointments for getting my hair and nails done. To me that's grooming, which I do regardless. Unless it's in preparation for a date or something that fills my soul, I don't usually cook. It's helpful in advance to know what takes from you and what gives or revives some aspect of your being.

Most importantly, sabbath is unplugging from the workday. I don't schedule client appointments. I've intentionally structured my professional life around my personal sabbath day. I refresh those key areas of my life and do things that pour into me. I nurture my body, mind, spirit, emotions, and personal relationships.

In taking care of my body, I can sleep later if I need more rest. I almost always do a workout for my back, which is part of my ongoing self-care. Or maybe when the weather's good, I enjoy my own company on a walk.

In caring for my mind and emotions, I may recite affirmations, journal, or do whatever connects me to my thoughts. To refresh my spirit, I spend a little extra time in my devotions or reading the word. Because I'm social, I'll usually meet a friend for coffee, lunch, or phone someone I haven't talked to in a while. Sometimes I'll write a card to a friend or send a text.

Because I do what is restful for me, I joyfully look forward to my weekly sabbath. It's a regular cyclical pulling away for restoration and refreshment. As my awareness changes, my self-care can also change. Deeper self-care allows you to continue searching out the best-for-you practices for regular and cyclical rest.

For Your Consideration

1. Can you envision how applying the principle of the sabbath can refresh and revitalize your life?
2. Which area of your being (body, mind, spirit, emotions, personal relationships) most needs refreshing? Create a plan to revitalize that area this week.
3. What steps will you take to incorporate sabbath rest into your day? What regular, cyclical habit can you tie to moments of self-care?

4 Boundaries

In a modern-day study[1], teachers took a group of school-aged children at their regularly scheduled recess time to two different but similar playgrounds. The essential difference between the two was the presence of a fence bordering the area on one playground, but not the other. The children on the playground with a fence remained near the teachers. In contrast, the children playing on the fenced playground moved away from the teachers and explored up to the fence, climbed on it, and sometimes even tried to get around it.

---

[1] [https://www.asla.org/awards/2006/studentawards/282.html]

I surmise that these children had a greater experience of security and autonomy when they had a clear sense of the outer limits. This study highlights the premise that borders, or boundaries, provide a sense of security which enables freedom to flourish.

Boundaries help us define who we are and who we are not. They help us remain healthy in our relationships with self and others. They keep good things in and harmful things out. Healthy, purposeful, clear boundaries protect our hearts, minds, physical bodies, and environments.

Setting healthy boundaries requires self-awareness. One can begin growing in self-awareness by monitoring your feelings in certain situations or with various people. Pay attention to your body and notice your physical cues. Ask yourself questions. What am I feeling? Am I anxious? Angry? Emotional? Exhausted? Name your feelings. What is it about this interaction, this individual, or this circumstance that makes me uncomfortable? Naming your feelings engages personal agency, the ability to control your responses to circumstances, events, and people. Self-awareness improves your clarity to know where you may need to form a boundary.

You may love visits from your family or

friends. But if they dominate your time, or they drain you emotionally, you might set a limit on how long a visit can last or where the visit occurs. A reasonable boundary lets you enjoy a visit while allowing you the freedom to control your time and energy. Expressing a boundary might sound like, "I'd love to see you. I have two hours I can devote exclusively to you at such and such a time."

Setting limits that protect your time, and access to you physically, spiritually, mentally, or emotionally, protects your soul and is a practice of self-care. Think of a boundary not only as a strategy to keep things out, but a method to maintain the integrity of what's inside. You are inside.

A common distortion or misuse of boundaries is when they're created to control or manipulate the actions of others. An awareness of self includes knowing what is and is not yours to manage. The thoughts, behaviors, or reactions of anyone else is not yours to do.

Using building materials as an analogy, consider what you might need in different situations. Does it need to be firm, like concrete, pliable, like rubber, or perforated, like mesh? For example, you may not mind somebody being in close physical proximity. You hold your children close, lean in toward your confidant, or hold hands with your lover. You might be a person who likes people close to you when you speak with them. However, that closeness may not carry over with people you don't know as well. Some folks feel uncomfortable being closer than three feet. If you step closer, they will probably back up to maintain the amount of space they need to feel safe.

Think about how your boundary is affected when you're in the presence of an unfriendly neighbor, or a person you view as a threat, or someone who has hurt you. You are probably keeping yourself out of reach. You automatically want more distance, and your boundary can be much firmer — concrete with spikes on top!

We may run into a toxic person in a public setting. Your boundary may be to keep moving rather than stop and risk an unhealthy interaction. Be clear with yourself as to your own acceptable rules of engagement. Don't violate yourself. Keep in mind that you can change your boundaries as people or dynamics change. Those whom you trust today may break that trust. You would be justified in erecting a boundary to protect yourself and limit or cut off their access to you. Conversely, someone who has hurt you in the past may sincerely repent and seek to restore. You may eventually change your boundary with that person.

We can apply boundaries in many other ways. As we mentioned earlier, you may need to erect boundaries around your time. This could apply to any person or circumstance that seeks to impose their agendas, needs, or undue pressure on you. This can occur at work, in volunteer positions, or even among dear friends. Their agendas may be completely innocent. If accepting tasks and responsibilities causes you to feel resentment or overwhelmed, you may need to limit when you're available. Choose temporary discomfort over long term resentment.

Self-awareness allows you to become attuned to what you do and don't like, do and don't want to do, and with whom you do and don't want to spend time. The more self-aware you are, the easier it will be to see where boundaries can and should be formed. If you find yourself in a situation that is untenable, ask yourself, what do I need to protect my freedom and peace of mind in this situation? Just as the strength and composition of boundaries can vary, so can the types of boundaries.

Types of Boundaries

Let's look at some of the most common ones. You

may choose to avoid situations that trigger unpleasant memories or cause stress and anxiety. If you know a certain relative always tries to mock you, embarrass you, or throw you under the bus, you might forgo family get-togethers when that relative attends. You may need to protect your time or mental health or physical body. You could also need boundaries for your privacy, such as how much personal information you're willing to share or express a standard as to how you expect to be addressed.

You can erect spiritual boundaries. Maybe you've chosen to express your faith or have a belief paradigm that differs from that which your family tradition dictates. Though that is your personal decision, a flexible or perforated boundary may better enable continued relationship.

Financial boundaries allow you to determine your budget. How you spend, or save your money, how you choose to invest, or how much and to whom you loan money.

Sexual boundaries protect your right to consent, where and how you want to be touched, in what way and by whom. Remember, a boundary guards the outside and protects the inside. A boundary could be abstaining from sex on the first date, or until your wedding night. The healthiest boundaries are informed by values and priorities.

Boundaries at work may take the form of keeping evenings and weekends open for family. A boundary lets you decide how much overtime you'll accept. It may look like declining extra hours that don't fit your plans. You may even turn down positions or promotions that conflict with your priorities.

Physical boundaries can be the most difficult to erect. If your physical body, your space, or property is being invaded or mistreated, an absolute physical boundary is necessary. We usually establish physical boundaries for protection. The violation of physical boundaries can be complicated.

By way of example, for an individual who's battered, it's already difficult to protect themselves. It's hard to set up a boundary and harder still to follow through if the boundary is breached. A protective order is a misnomer because it's only enforceable if it's violated. The violator gets in trouble only if they break it. It doesn't really keep anybody away and doesn't really protect, though it may be a necessary start.

It often means that the violated person must leave a particular environment and venture into an unknown space when they already feel highly vulnerable. Leaving a relationship is not so cut-and-dry. When people say, "Just leave! Why won't you leave?" Getting to that place psychologically is complex. There is enormous loss tied to exiting a relationship. Many times children are involved. Is the victim financially able to leave? Is the abuser also the primary provider? An exit strategy requires the careful weighing of many factors, but it can be done.

Dealbreakers and Tricky Boundaries

Some boundaries can be nonnegotiable, such as what type of behavior you will not tolerate in a relationship or in marriage. This means if somebody crosses the deal-breaking boundary, you must make good on the consequences you've outlined. A wife may decide she will not tolerate abusive language or being demeaned. Married spouses may refuse to tolerate cheating, or they may choose to involve a therapist and restore the marriage.

Financial boundaries in marriage or committed relationships may include personal spending caps. Upon reaching a certain dollar amount, they must consult their partner before proceeding with a purchase.

It bears repeating that boundaries are not

meant to control or manipulate other people. However, as outlined above, they can help create the framework that allows you to be with those whom you choose. They are the proverbial fenced playground within which lies freedom and security.

Let's look at a boundary that has to do with your gifting. I'll use myself as an example to clarify what I mean. One of my boundary issues has to do with my inclination to help others. At the core of who I am, my "gift bundle" is a mix of passion, wisdom, discernment, and empathy. With my training, I have a lot of skill in that space that I'm more than happy to share. The sun shines on my gift bundle, but it also casts a shadow.

Because I have a natural capacity for compassion, I tend to step in with caregiving or advice when I haven't been asked. This is the shadow side. Being aware of that tendency means I must ask myself some questions. Am I stepping into a place where I wasn't invited? Am I giving more that I can comfortably give? After giving in this way, will I feel depleted or resentful? Am I taking care of myself? Where is the boundary line?

Self-awareness is key to understanding your own boundaries. Pay close attention to your needs, your weaknesses, and those places where you want to grow. Through my self-awareness, I see places where I need to exercise boundaries. I take them into consideration regarding how and where I move, and what I ingest. I consider what I take in mentally (by what I think and listen to), and through my eyes (by what I allow myself to look at), and in how I treat my body.

You may need to exercise boundaries with your own parents or loved ones. They probably intend good for you, but you reserve the right to say what doesn't work for you or your schedule. An example of parental boundaries occurred with my mom. She wanted to come up a few days before the due date of our first child to be present when the baby came. I wasn't willing to do that with the first baby. If it came late, I'd be waiting for the baby with my mom. Waiting was already stressful. People called to ask so often, I just answered the phone, "No baby yet! Hello?"

Since I didn't want Mom waiting with me, I suggested she wait until I was officially in labor. She respected that boundary. In the meantime, because this occurred pre-internet, she made a chart with all the flights and packed a bag. At our go ahead, she was on the next flight and arrived that evening in time to go to the hospital with us. In her era, she had not seen her own children born and was very excited to share in the birth of her grandchild.

Mom stayed for about two weeks. When she was getting ready to leave, I remember I didn't want her to go. Maybe I was a little nervous about taking care of a newborn on my own. She said, "I came to take care of *my* baby. I didn't take care of *your* baby. *You've* been taking care of your baby." Just that one last statement was so impactful, so profound, so empowering, and very "boundaried."

Unclear boundaries can reflect one's perception of their own value, security, or significance. There was a time when an unconscious pull compelled me to give in to a request to keep people in relationship with me. As I grew in self-awareness, so did the understanding of my value. As I grew in understanding my value, I was better able to see where I needed reasonable boundaries. In all cases where I exerted reasonable boundaries, I still maintained those relationships. They were healthier and contained a freedom that had been obscured by resentment or regret.

An incident in my personal life caused me to think more seriously about my boundaries. It took place inside a quiet public setting. One person in the room was intoxicated and getting very loud.

Given the normally quiet and peaceful environment, this was inappropriate. My automatic response was a soft, "Shhhhh." Instead of being respectful, the loud person got louder. They began yelling and swearing at me. I had to pass many people to leave the room while they continued their tirade. In my embarrassment and anger, I wanted to yell and cuss them out, matching their energy. Thankfully, I was able to tearfully hold it together, but that event changed how I handled that relationship. I had to realize that their overreaction had little to nothing to do with me. Thereafter, I developed very strong boundaries regarding future interactions with that individual.

In this instance, setting a physical and emotional boundary isn't up for discussion, and their approval isn't required. This one is for my protection, and they don't have a say in that. After examining the dynamic for patterns and my contribution to it, I recognized that not only was I not exempt from the other person's pattern of behavior, but that I had allowed it. I no longer put myself in harm's way. My boundary protects me. Now my interactions in this relationship are managed, peaceful, intentional, and emotionally safe.

It didn't change their behavior; it did change mine. I still deeply care about them. Now I show up when I want to, not based on some duty I feel. When I show up, they're happy to see, and I leave before they get on my nerves.

Having boundaries colors the way I celebrate with my family. When I want a party to be a certain way and maintain a certain tone, I choose to avoid inviting unpredictable elements that drain me or unnecessarily distract my mind. As the ringleader, and person who loves taking care of people, I need to gauge the room and keep the party going. Boundaries protect the joyful atmosphere and my emotional state so I can be present for my guests and those I want to celebrate. I've learned that if certain people are there, I can't be sure what they're bringing. Then I'm weighed down thinking, "Where is so and so? Have they had too much alcohol? Is this the moment where it turns from being hilarious and gregarious to mean?" Babysitting guests is exhausting. That isn't why I throw a party.

Enforcing Boundaries

You may need some assistance in keeping your boundaries intact. Especially those where there is the greatest amount of resistance. A family member or spouse backing you up can be the difference between the boundary being respected or overrun. In my family, we checked in with our boys. I usually initiated with a question like, "How are we doing in our relationship?"

On this one day, thinking we were good, my then ten-year-old son surprised me. "You know, you're doing pretty well. You're a pretty good mom... except that it really gets hard to punish myself."

When I asked what he meant, he explained. If losing his video games is the punishment we've decided, he would invite his friend over to play with him. With his friend there, my son knew I'd make an exception. They knew I'm big on making memories, being social, and that I love having people over to my house. Now here he is saying, *I know how to get around your punishments — by inviting a friend over.*

Kudos to him for trying to do the right thing! Despite his honesty in telling me this, my clever son later circumvented punishment and invited his friend over again. He thought he'd gotten around his punishment... until his father came home.

"Hey son, what's your friend doing here? Aren't you on restriction?" Eric asked. Our son's tactic didn't work at all on his dad. He packed up my son's friend and took him home. That's what should have happened. I needed Eric to back me up and help enforce the boundary I set.

Some boundaries are more challenging to guard. Are you giving time, finances, or resources beyond your capacity? You may need to create a boundary about what you can and can't give. When some need comes up from family or friends that taps your resources, wisdom encourages us to think it over. You may have long-held triggers and need to consider the request and the impact for a couple of days before you can even respond. A reminder phrase such as, "Poor planning on your part does not constitute an emergency on my part," can help you remain objective while you weigh the pros and cons. For what reasons might you say yes? If your natural inclination is to say yes, it's helpful to know why and under what circumstances. Using your self-awareness, how do you feel about giving your resources? Are you freely giving, or do you feel pressured to give? If you give, will you feel resentful? Some folks give only what they can comfortably afford to lose if they are not repaid.

Most of us don't mind helping somebody in a crisis. However, some "emergency" situations are the obvious last-stage development that could have been addressed months before it reached epic proportions, such as shut off notices, repossession, eviction, and foreclosure. If you know someone who constantly needs financial rescue, your impulse may be to drop everything and give them exactly what they're asking for, because it's hard to have someone disappointed in you. Possibly you need to say no or suggest other options.

Offer to help them create a budget or share the contact information of a trusted financial counselor. Maintaining healthy financial boundaries protects you and encourages them to consider making positive changes by getting past destructive habits.

Deciding Which Boundaries Apply

When I understood how a lack of boundaries affected me, deciding to erect firmer ones and enforcing them became easier. Keep in mind that a boundary is only as good as you make it. If you say no to some circumstance, then you must mean no and be willing to defend that boundary. People don't like not having full access to you, your time, or your space. If anybody can badger you into changing it, like kids often do, or if you let them wear you down and you give in, then you didn't mean it. And by caving in, you've taught them how to get around it.

If you're wondering how to use boundaries,

ask yourself these questions. What is your reason for setting it up? Are you trying to control another person's behavior? What are you maintaining or protecting—peace, safety, harmony, or yourself? You may reach the same conclusion; the result may be erecting the same boundary. What matters is the motivation. Be clear on what it's for and why you're erecting it. Even though folks on the other side may not like it, even when they're done in love, they will respect it.

You decide how solid, soft, or perforated it must be. Just don't remove it. Getting it just right usually involves some trial and error. Be judicious in how many iron-clad boundaries you set up. As you become more self-aware, you will have stronger, healthier boundaries.

For Your Consideration

1. Can you find at least one area in your life where you already have a boundary in place? Has that boundary been strengthened or weakened since it was erected? Write down the consequences that must follow if it is violated.
2. For any boundaries that you have in place, or plan to erect, write down your reasons

for them. What do you gain or protect by having these boundaries?
3. Listen to your body and pay attention to your cues. These indicate places where some boundaries can be helpful. After an interaction, check in with yourself. What emotions do you feel? When a certain name comes up on your phone, how do react?

MENTAL

5 Perfectionism and Fear

Wouldn't it be nice if you gave your best to a project or even to your appearance and let it go at that? Chasing after perfection is like running after the iridescent-winged unicorn. A person can exert tremendous effort to catch something that doesn't exist. Simply stated, perfect doesn't exist. It's an elusive standard for one's body, in your thoughts and in relationships. It doesn't exist in business strategies or practices, not in people, and not even in nature. No matter what area you choose, there will always be room for improvement, for better communication, a healthier, stronger body, or a more beneficial thought life.

Even in those spaces where you might be tempted to argue that perfect does exist (say, rocket science or brain surgery), it is fleeting. There will always be more innovation. New improvements. Upgrades. Add-ons and reformulations. If perfect existed, there would be no evolution to the next thing. Whatever the thing is, there's always room for growth.

So, why do we strive for perfection? For this discussion, perfectionism is distinguished from a standard of excellence. I'm referring particularly of the psychological, emotional, and relational toll that perfectionism can take.

A perfectionistic personality can develop from factors such as invalidating early childhood experiences, or as a trauma response. It is often a response to poor self-esteem, feelings of inadequacy, and anxiety. The *pursuit* of perfectionism — whether in a person's looks or accomplishments — serves to temper these feelings. And when perfectionism is projected upon others, it presents as controlling.

Perfection is outward focused, meaning you're measuring yourself against some outside influence. You have a perspective of what it looks like from somewhere, and you're bound and determined to reach it. Who set the standard that you're pursuing?

Many of the clients I've worked with who've

suffered with anxiety and almost always felt they were failing. This was often because they were under the constant distortion that they were not good enough in some way; that there was a standard they couldn't meet. The ubiquitous question, "What if I'm not enough?" is at the root of many of our unspoken fears. The fear of failure, of not meeting someone's standard, of being judged. A fear of having to show up a certain way… not pretty enough, smart enough, capable enough, strong enough, etc.

Isn't it a good thing to pursue higher standards? Of course! Cultivating a growth mindset and delivering our best efforts are good things. But if you're constantly reaching for perfection, you'll notice you never quite catch the bar because it's always rising. It's always rising because it isn't tethered to anything real. Who decides what is perfect? Who qualified them to be the arbiter of perfection? If the pursuit of elusive perfection is distorted, then one is equally distorted if you believe you've achieved it. There's a distorted rigidity to perfectionism that isn't practical. Perfect would be a ceiling, and once achieved there's nowhere else to go.

The difference between perfectionists and pursuers of excellence is that perfectionists who focus on achieving flawlessness often miss the satisfaction that comes from putting in a good effort, or the excitement of an unexpected positive outcome. The unfortunate twist is that they often accomplish less because fear chokes out creativity, prevents a good start, or inhibits progress. In this chapter we'll focus on self-care for those who find themselves continually striving for perfection or those who identify as perfectionists. I believe there's a more healthy, practical, and freeing way to move as our best selves.

Ways We Strive

We may be triggered to chase after perfectionism in our looks or in the shape of our bodies. In my lifetime, plastic surgery has bloomed into a sixteen-billion-dollar industry. That translates into a lot of people who don't like the contours of their nose and view myriad other body parts as less than "perfect." So, to "improve" on our design, big bucks are spent altering our bodies. I refer not only to clinical expertise, and personal experience, but to my Christian faith for perspective on these matters. Nowhere in the Bible does it describe what the perfect person looked like, not in features, body type, size, or the length and texture of their hair. We may think of Jesus as perfect. The Bible describes him as being average in looks, so there was something that wasn't perfect about how he looked! Even when the Bible highlights people who were particularly good-looking, that detail served their larger story; and even then, their appearance is not described.

So what is this mythical standard so many people try to meet? If there was truly a perfect form, it would be the same standard for all people everywhere. It wouldn't change in every generation or be dependent on where you are in the world.

When I was in college, I held a firmly distorted view of my body, and thus was always trying to lose weight. A beloved elder woman who hailed from Barbados always told me, "Eat, child! You'd have a hard time getting a man on the island." In her island culture, men like their women bigger. According to her, a man with a skinny wife is looked down upon. It means he's not taking care of her, he's not feeding her well, and he's not a good provider. They would tell him, "You need to put some meat on those bones!"

Those looks we strive for, do surgery for, and starve our bodies for, are the results of targeted marketing trends determined by researchers who have studied the fears and desires of the market. Who decided what the perfect body should look like? I, too, have been a victim of those decades-old marketing strategies. I don't judge anyone who does those things for the purpose of improvement, for purposes of health, even if you decide that's what you want to do to look better for yourself. Plastic surgery has a place if you need it or choose it. I simply encourage you to understand by whose standards are you measuring yourself? Are you masking a deeply felt inadequacy or are you consciously choosing certain methods as self-care?

After a cancer diagnosis, I benefited from plastic surgery and even went on to have optional procedures. I'm not under the delusion that I'm moving toward perfection, as much as restoration. Those procedures accomplished what I couldn't with my own efforts, to replace in a manner what was lost. However, it made me aware of how one can carry a distorted view of themselves toward a "fix" without knowing that their true motivation may be a futile pursuit of a non-existent standard of perfection, rather than a conscious choice for personal betterment.

If the cosmetic surgery industry numbers mentioned earlier surprise you, the weight loss industry makes it pale in comparison. It topped seventy-two billion just a few years ago. I know I'm not alone. Millions have participated in measuring themselves against a standard set by others, the mythical "they."

The perfect body is a myth. There will always be a few pounds or inches to go. More strength to be gained, bigger muscles to be had, more ripped abs to strive for, or more flawless skin to be chased.

We want to engage our projects, tasks, habits, and relationships with humility. We want to bring our best efforts forward, knowing that all of it is a work in progress. Innovation continues, bodies will change, relationships will evolve, and we will grow. Let's gain joy and satisfaction in the now.

Better Than Perfect

On Instagram, I follow a classy British woman who does fashion videos for women over fifty. When she started sharing bits of her story, she wasn't just a gorgeous woman wearing beautiful clothes. She was a woman who helped her followers understand how she got to the place where she's able to say, "Let me help you feel this way in your clothes." She let us in on her journey to freedom of expression.

The other day she had something on that

was really becoming. And I didn't have another word. I couldn't find a flaw. I commented, "Perfection!" Did I just put a standard on her? If that's just a word you use in the vernacular, like it is for me, that's fine. But if you identify it as a standard to be achieved, that's different.

Pursuing excellence shifts the focus away from perfection and produces sweeter fruit from the same effort. Excellence means, I'm taking all that I have today and doing my best in this situation. Most likely that will be really good! Excellence leaves room for competence, humility, and growth. Even the Almighty after completing each phase of creation said, *"And it was good!"* Not only does excellence allow for evolution and innovation, but it also allows you to feel satisfaction.

If you create the perfect garment and it's truly perfect, you're done! But if fashions change the following year, new garments will be created. With excellence, you create the best garment given your resources and knowledge at the time. The following year when styles change again, you create another excellent garment.

If you want to provide the best product or present your idea or yourself, in the best way that you know how, please do! However, make your standard contextual. Even on a bad day, excellence is achievable. Giving your very best with the resources that you have in any given day is excellence.

Setting the Standard

Recently, I met with girlfriends in Miami. They were looking edgy and sharp, wearing heels and toting tiny little bags. When I started comparing, I decided the dress I had packed explicitly for this outing wasn't perfect for me. Sometimes, I don't want to have to carry a big, old heavy bag. Being prepared with a cane and extra shoes and all that I need, I get weary, believe me. I wanted to look like somebody else in that situation. The crossroads I stood in was deciding who was going to set the standard for me.

Although I wanted to look edgy and sharp too, I could still be excellent. This is the mindset I took to this situation because pursuing excellence is self-awareness 101 — doing for myself what I need to do. I didn't want to wear the gingham dress because I thought it looked too "sweet."

Until I remembered there's a reason why I packed that dress. It didn't require me tugging on it to make sure I was covered. As an A-line dress, it accentuates my best feature which is my waist. It's lightweight, had pockets, and looks great with either sneakers or sandals. I could move freely in the heat in my body in that dress. I knew it was the right dress to wear. I was comfortable and cute. Everywhere I went people complimented my outfit. I accepted who I was in that dress. Was it the perfect dress? For that occasion, it was excellent! For church, no. The dress itself is not perfect.

If I had externalized the standard, letting comparison set the tone for how I needed to show up, I wouldn't have been able to be present in the experience and relate freely with my friends. I would have suffered trying to keep up with the girls. I wouldn't have been free to enjoy brunching at the cool place with my dear friends. It is so automatic to do this externalizing and comparing.

So why did I have to go through all that? What's the distortion that needs to be exposed? The clinician in me says, if you really want to care for yourself, get to the root of the fear. What does your perfectionism solve? Not only what are your areas of perfectionism, but what's at the core of it? Mine was that if the curtain is peeled back, they're going to find out that I'm not all that. That I'm a fraud, or not as pretty, confident, or smart as they think I am. When I let go of the fear of not meeting some external standard, I let go of showing up as I think people expect.

Freedom is my standard. What produces the most freedom? What allows me the freedom to show up in my space as the person I am right now? My standard frees me to be fully present in the moment. And it's my responsibility to guard it. My preference. My standard. Practical and free. That knowledge and awareness is self-care.

For Your Consideration

1. In what areas are you striving to reach a standard that isn't yours? What do you really need?
2. When you remind yourself to pursue excellence, what changes in your thinking? What differences do you feel in your body?
3. In what areas of frustration are you comparing yourself to someone else? What happens when you let go of that?

6 Dreams & Aspirations

I was a stay-at-home mom with my boys during their childhood. As they got older, I began to think more about how to refocus my life. In the context of being a homemaker, my dreams had taken a turn that differed from the years before parenthood. As a wife and mother, my dreams had become largely situational, practical, and necessary. I dreamed of having all the laundry done, having an organized home, or getting everyone where they needed to be. My husband and I made that choice before we got married. Being so young, we didn't have a good understanding of either the privileges it allowed, or the sacrifices required.

Many people dream of being free to have the

choice to care for their home and raise their families, and there are just as many for whom that would never be their choice. This isn't a statement about the efficacy of how one parents. It's an exploration of the importance of having dreams and aspirations no matter your context. If you're blessed to keep living, your context will likely change many times. The members that make up your household will change, your body will change, circumstances and responsibilities will change. Life will happen. The events that catalyzed my need to begin dreaming again were the loss of my mother, a second cancer diagnosis, and my sons maturing into their own lives.

Sensing it was time to show up in my life in a different capacity, I asked myself, what were the things I used to dream of being and doing? Were those things still relevant? What could be new? What current experiences and skills can be expanded or refined? I prayed to the Lord, "Will you help me? I don't remember how to dream."

The first dream I acted upon was to apply to grad school. I was accepted into a Clinical Counseling program, graduated several years later, and began working at a private counseling practice. Once I stepped into those aspirations and they were realized, I noticed that different opportunities created more dreams. Through these new experiences, the Lord sensitized me to dreaming again.

International travel really opened me to seeing outside of myself. A paradigm shift moved me from my practical and insular vision to a more expanded, yet personal one. The world is so much bigger than a laundry room and a house. The privilege of travel showed me that whatever your context, all people want the same things. Our core human longings are to have love, belonging, purpose, significance, safety, and understanding. International travel moved me from a local personal understanding to a larger vision: how my home, family, neighborhood, and country fit into a larger context and how we work out our humanity in those spaces.

Making Room for Dreams

When opportunities arise, allow them to spark new visions. Those sparks may come in the form of suggestions, questions, or simply observations. You don't have to qualify yourself before accepting or stepping into new experiences. Initially, I was guilty of this. Instead, ask a different question. What happens if you just run with it? What's the best that could happen? What if this is the first step into a new adventure or at worst, a new learning? Even though challenge can be scary, if you're open to new things, courageously ask yourself what doors will open if you do this thing? This is supported by Hebrews 10:35 which says, "So, do not throw away this confident trust in the Lord. Remember the great reward it brings you!" I believe that by putting your trust in God, He brings opportunities about.

For example, when I asked God, "Can you help me dream? What do I want to do? Is there something I want to experience? Is there a place where I can leave a mark?" Doors were opened and my awareness was raised to recognize the occasions He brought to me.

One long-held dream was to skydive. I sensed new things were on the other side of this adventure. Wanting to conquer a fear of moving into the unknown, He brought a person into my circle who pushed me through my own procrastination. The day I planned to jump, the instructors noticed a limp and asked about it. My instructor pulled me aside to gain more information and prepare me for the possibility that my jump would be canceled. After hearing my spirit of determination, and what this jump meant to me, he said he had an idea. He switched the order of the jump and planned a different landing for me that wouldn't put my leg at risk. To this day, my skydiving experience is truly meaningful. It reminded me of my strength and provided many metaphors of courage, perseverance, and salvation – unlike anything I had experienced before. It's another example in my life story that reminds me of my own fierceness and of God's intervention. The individual that pushed things along is no longer in my life, but God used them to reveal a higher level of strength that only He knew I'd need. Only He knew what dividends pursuing that dream would pay in the long run.

Dreams can be revealed through crisis. Personal life catastrophes can shake you up in such a way that you must reenvision yourself. With a bone cancer diagnosis as a teenager, I assumed I was going to die. All statistics pointed in that direction. I didn't have a dream or any vision for my future. I only wanted to be inspiring to others by dying well. And then against all odds I survived! I remember thinking, "I need to come up with a new plan! I guess I'll go to college!"

Another crisis was my mother's early death. Without a role model to provide an example or guidance, I had to create my own vision. Who do I dream myself to be?

After going through a crisis, people use the phrase, "new normal." We tend to gloss over the gravity of that statement. It requires great effort to embrace that something unforeseen is now normal for you. After cancer, my "new normal" was mitigating various things for my body so I could be present and enjoy the main event. I had to learn to honor the person I had become. That meant rather than being angry when my body didn't allow me to do what I wanted, choosing to give her whatever she needed: the comfortable shoes, the pain reliever, the cane, or rest. It's not a new normal anymore. It can be wearisome and inconvenient at times. But I've accepted my own story and allowed myself to embrace it.

Most people have negative thoughts and narratives on occasion. By understanding how they limit creativity and block dreaming, one can learn to reframe and reprocess those limiting statements.

It's important to pay attention to the weight of the words being used. Limiting statements and limiting beliefs can cut you off from your aspirations or dreams. Speak to yourself as you would someone you love and want to encourage.

To dream and reenvision yourself, first, you must process the crisis, the thing that took away your old normal. Who you were then and the loss of what is passing out of your life must be acknowledged. New normal is the process of making peace with the change and the new version you get to become as a result. There is great power and great freedom in this choice.

Dream Drivers

Sometimes, I'm concerned about making sure I'm not wasting all the work that God did to preserve me. I could have died a bunch of times. As people around me continue to die from cancer, I'm keenly aware I've survived it—twice! I've outlived a number of my relatives, including my parents, and lived beyond the age my mother was when she passed.

"Am I living up to why you kept me here?" I ask the Lord, fearing sometimes that I'm not worth the effort that God poured into me. Rather than seeing that as a place to be afraid or of failing God, I allow myself to be open, listening and watching for opportunities. Dreaming starts with self-awareness and curiosity. Ask yourself, what am I interested in? What are the things that make me who I am? Is there a greater purpose with which I want to align?

What could dreaming look like for you? Is your heart sensitive to where He might be leading?

Are you able to take risks and see coincidences or divine appointments?

Here's a great illustration. A nurse came to my home to draw my blood for an insurance policy during COVID-19. We both wore medical masks (as was proper at that time) and never saw each other's full faces. During our conversation, she said, "You have a lot to offer. You should do a podcast!"

"Yeah, I don't know," I said. "I've been thinking a lot about blogging."

"But you like to talk!" She already had me all figured out. "You should do a podcast." She took the time to pull out her phone and showed me a podcast app. "Just talk into your phone. You can do this." I had in mind to follow through on her advice. And what's interesting about dreams is that they don't follow a linear path. They can be ignited by conversation or random encounter. A suggestion was made, a crisis followed. Here's how the dream manifested.

My goddaughter passed away, and I took a leave of absence from clinical work. With the mission to process my grief, I went away. While spending time journaling, I'd get content from what I processed that day. "Podcasting" started with making and posting two- or three-minute videos on Facebook in the hope that sharing my grief process would be helpful to others. And people appreciated them.

During shelter-in-place, there were lots of virtual cocktail parties going on. Trying to keep things fun, Eric and I started something new. Whoever finished work first would try a new cocktail recipe, and we'd celebrate the end of the day. Just for fun, I decided to make a video about making cocktails. And people loved them.

Since I like talking, sharing, posting, and making cocktails, I wondered how to tie them together? And that evolved into *Tales from the Shaker*. The shaker is the person; the shaker is about events that shook me up. Things that made me rethink the status quo. A shaking event makes you see a new thing, try a new thing, or learn something about yourself–a passion, a revelation, or a new direction.

As the host, I welcome guests into my home, where we record and share food, and I make a cocktail or mocktail. At the end, we share a toast to our conversation. The podcasts capture more of me than anything else I do, even though the stories are about other people.

Dreaming gave me the bandwidth to entertain an idea and try something new. I asked a question, then noticed an opportunity. Who knew that bossy nurse would have such an effect on my life? We didn't see each other's faces until over a year later, and she's even been one of my podcast guests! Sharing personal stories is a risk for some, but I'm going to follow this to see where it goes. It's fun, and I'm still dreaming.

Box Free

A lot of us live in self-imposed boxes. Dreaming is another place for you to expand the boundaries of who you are. You don't have to dream of being famous, but you can if you like. Your dream is something that appeals to you, something you might be wishing for, that isn't currently a part of your life. It's something that you may aspire to become, or an evolving vision of what your future could look like. Dreams are those things that live in your head until you find a way to make them your reality.

Depending on your background, and what you've lived through, you may dream of having a safe home. Maybe you dream of visiting every continent. It could be a business startup. It may involve bettering the lives of children or solving a societal issue. What mark do you want to leave on the earth? What experiences would you like to create or have or share?

Pursuing your dreams is an important component of self-care. As your perspective expands, you may express your boundaries differently. The people with whom you interact may not respond with enthusiasm. Following your dream may affect your availability to them. This may mean fewer family meals, missed social time, increased travel, and shifting priorities. The people on the other side of that boundary may have an initial reaction. Some may be wholeheartedly supportive, and others may be less so.

By leaning into your ambitions, you also create space for others in your immediate circle to expand as well. Your days free of meal-making responsibilities may allow for another family member to step in and develop cooking skills or increase their culinary expertise.

Your new pursuit may affect your availability to extended family and friends. You may hear comments like, "If you're too busy for family, you're too busy," or, "We never see you anymore." Not everyone will be happy that you're pursuing your aspirations, especially when it takes away from time you used to spend together. When you pursue something new, you don't experience your own absence from the old habits, but others do. And the closer they are to you, the more they will notice your absence.

This is a good place to practice the pause and process your thoughts before responding. If it's within your ability, help them understand the importance this holds for you. Provide context. Then carry on.

Sky's the Limit

It's okay to aspire to more. By dreaming, you envision a more hopeful future. You honor yourself, your story, and your presence. Pursuing your dreams permits you to expand the spaces that you allow yourself to occupy. It opens you up, and your natural lane becomes broader. Dreaming is the playground of innovation, the in-between place before breaking through to reality. Everything you see on the earth was someone's dream first.

While pursuing your dreams, you've opened avenues for more information to come to you. New information brings exposure to new ideas and opportunities to investigate. How do you find out if you're an inventor or musically inclined? How do you know if you're the next great visionary, author, or artist? You must take that first tentative step, explore that "crazy" idea, and run with your dream to see where it leads.

Your dreams are yours. You own yourself, your mind, and your thoughts when you dream. You gain clarity on who you want to be, or feel you're supposed to be. Your dreams may require action at some point; just begin by pondering the possibilities. One of my sons used to sit on a big rock in the front yard. He'd climb on it and just sit there.

"What are you doing?" I'd ask.

"Sitting on the Wonder Rock, just wondering," he'd answer.

When is the last time you just sat and wondered? Over time, with responsibilities and busyness, life takes over. Those wonder-filled pauses drift away. We owe it to ourselves to take back our wondering.

Just as seedlings emerging from the soil are fragile, so are your dreams. You're not obligated to share them with anyone at this early stage. It's okay to protect them. Choose to reveal them only to those who can truly appreciate and encourage you to follow them. If you don't yet have those people, you can still move forward with the expectation that they're coming. Growth-minded, supportive, truth-tellers will find you. In the meantime, guard your dreams by not allowing others to take shots, minimize or tear them down. Your dreams are to fill you with hope—so let hope grow.

For Your Consideration

1. What are you curious about? Consider creating a list and looking into each one.
2. Like the Wonder Rock, what place is your go-to to just wonder?
3. Who has inspired you lately, or suggested something you can try? What happens if you just run with it?

7 Priorities

If I've noticed one thing in my practice, it's that many people, but particularly women put themselves last. Historically, women are encouraged to defer to others first to fulfill their roles in relationship. The ability to put others first is the measuring stick that determines whether you're a good daughter, a good partner, friend, or spouse. Thinking of others before ourselves is applauded.

Such thinking finds its roots in the Bible: to love your neighbor as yourself, to treat one another as more important than yourself, and making it a habit to serve one another. This is also found in many cultures around the world. That command is not flawed. It is important to treat others well. My standard is based on these biblical directives, which I believe to be true. However, more than one thing can be true at the same time.

When we think of loving others, we do others a disservice when we don't bring our full selves to that space from a fortified position. I'm not suggesting we show up selfishly as in, "I'm the most important person in the whole world!" I view showing up for ourselves as loving, realistic, and necessary. For example, if you have children, when you feed them, don't you also eat? When you put your children to bed, at some point, you also go to sleep. You drink your own water and stretch your own muscles. You must take care of the body that's taking care of everybody else. If you only feed the children without ever feeding yourself, you will not be at your best and your whole being, as well as those you serve, will suffer.

The natural order of the world makes us an essential part of the whole, like a spoke in a wheel. Prioritizing yourself is essential, not selfish. Learning how to prioritize that which strengthens us is necessary to properly manage our responsibilities and create space for joy.

Put Yourself on the List

You're born into a world and live with people who take care of you. After learning to take care of yourself, you take on roles. Each of us becomes responsible for how we live out our personhood. Somehow, over the course of time, you may find you've stopped prioritizing your needs but continued executing your roles. The danger of prioritizing responsibilities ahead of what you need, is that over time, you become less effective over those responsibilities. Maintaining your personal priorities requires acknowledging what your needs are.

When you wake up in the morning, you likely tend to other people in your household or put your attention on other tasks. Have you considered what you need? What if you woke up and prioritized yourself by spending a moment acknowledging, appreciating and being grateful for the fact that you woke up? When you end your day, what does that look like? When we are at our best, our most healthy, we close the day in a manner that sets us up for a good night's rest. Restorative rest sets the foundation for the following morning.

For instance, one person's end-of-day-routine might include sipping a cup of calming tea before shutting down the house. Winding down could include a shower, applying lotion or reading until you start to doze. Some may tense and release muscles and practice deep breathing. Others may complete a series of stretches before retiring for the evening. One habit I've found helpful is having a notepad by the bed. Usually my mind is still swirling with thoughts. By writing them down, it gets them off my mind. I can trust my notepad to hold those thoughts for me until I pick them up the next day.

The end of the day routine is about preparing to get the most restorative sleep. Each step is a cue to your body and mind that you're ending the day. We know intuitively that children must prepare for bed in a certain order. We usually bathe them, have some quiet play time, and read them a story. We know how important it is to relax the atmosphere and calm the body and mind, so that they're able to fall asleep. For most adults, we must reenvision our bedtime routine. It's part of our self-awareness and self-care to figure out what works best for us.

Everyone will occasionally fall off their routines. Life is full of interruptions. It's simply a matter of getting back to it. Routines don't have to be perfect, but they are valuable self-care.

In my profession, when a new client comes on board, part of the assessment includes an inquiry regarding the general condition of the client's health. The quality, consistency, and disruptions in sleeping and eating patterns provide significant information as to overall physical, mental, and emotional functioning.

Just like going to bed prepares your mind and body for rest, waking up prepares your body and mind for action. When we create these patterns of waking and sleeping, it gives our brain the best opportunity for our happy chemicals to activate. [2] You want to do those things that naturally allow for dopamine and serotonin to be released in the brain: get enough sleep, eat well, meditate, and exercise. Dopamine provides a temporary sense of pleasure. Serotonin helps sustain the longevity of that mood booster. Equally valuable is how you begin your morning, and having a morning routine will set the tone and posture for your day.

A common experience of those who struggle with anxiety is the feeling of being hit with it as soon as they're aware of being awake. One way to get ahead of that is through deep breathing, stretching the body, and tensing and releasing muscles. As the physical symptoms wane, praying over yourself or saying affirmations into the calm space before getting up is helpful. I start my day by changing into my workout clothes, which I keep by the bed. I do my devotions and journal while having

---

[2] https://www.health.harvard.edu/mind-and-mood/dopamine-the-pathway-to-pleasure

coffee or tea. This may sound like a lot of steps, but none of them take more than about five minutes.

A round of deep breathing takes roughly sixty seconds. You don't have to spend twenty minutes in ritual meditation for this to be effective. But if that's important to incorporate into your morning, by all means, do it!

Breaks in the Day

Something else I often do is tie mindful breathing to something that's going to happen anyway. On my way to the office, I prioritized times of refreshing. I spent time deep breathing. At work I prayed over my office before clients arrived. When I returned home, before entering the house, I spent two minutes meditating in the car with the radio turned down, putting a cap on the workday. This helped me avoid bringing home unresolved things from work and prepared me for an evening at home.

Altogether, there were four times every day that I chose for myself: As part of my bedtime routine, my waking routine, driving to work and returning home from work. In total, five or six minutes. When I fall off the routine I notice in my overall peace and calm; I see a difference in my attitude and perspective. When COVID-19 happened, and I was no longer driving to the office, I lost some of that rhythm and had to find it again. My days flow better when I maintain it. My morning rituals put me in touch with greater principles—my well-being and values—that I want to guide my day. I'm still looking at my calendar and approaching my day with an attitude of gratitude, but my routine elevates my well-being above the tasks of the day.

Things that are most important to you are sustainable when you align them with your values. The importance of your rituals—many that you may not even realize you have—is that they're indicators of how well you're doing. These placekeepers are the first thing to fall off when something's awry.

You don't have to add on a bunch of time to an already busy day to make yourself a priority. You're going to have a meal, brush your teeth, travel to work or the store or an appointment. The point is to capture moments for yourself by tying deep breathing, drinking water, or moving your body to one of those times. Your days won't always flow smoothly like a continuous stream; circumstances and events will interrupt the current.

This happens to me too. With extensive traveling, playdates with my granddaughter, and different things, I fall off my routines. I'm in it more days than not, which is excellent. When I wake up, if I don't do the things I like to do then, I may not find time during the day. Relieving tension with breathing or muscle tensing and releasing can be done in the car or waiting in line somewhere or between appointments. These moments benefit me and take nothing from anyone else, nor do they reduce my availability. Be on the lookout for moments where you can be fully present for yourself.

I love that people are talking about self-care with their friends, on talk shows and social media, as well as becoming more aware and more intentional. However, it seems cheapened when it's reduced to getting a massage or taking a bath. These activities fly under the banner of, *I do this for myself; therefore, this is my self-care.* Were you doing them before "self-care" became a thing? Don't stop doing those things if you enjoy them. You don't need to justify them.

Self-care is much deeper than physical hygiene. I'd like to see your understanding of self-care expanded, so you prioritize working on your emotional life and learning how to communicate with yourself and others. I'd like to see you prioritize forgiving yourself and others regarding the things that have happened to you. I want you to prioritize therapy, the process of grieving, and those places where you disappointed or dismissed yourself. I desire for you to prioritize each facet of self-care covered in this book. When you do, what you've gained will positively affect how you choose to work out your days, weeks, months, and years.

Intentional Body Moves

Something will shift in your allocation of time if or when you decide to include moving your body as part of your self-care. What seems to work best for many people is starting small, being consistent, and building over time.

Let's say you've never worked out. You set a goal to work out an hour a day five days a week. It's great if you do it! By starting with too grand a picture, you may be setting yourself up for failure. Thus, instead of being grateful for what you did accomplish, you might be berating yourself for what you didn't do.

If it hasn't been a part of your life, it would be more realistic to start small and build with a focus on consistency. What if you just stand up from your desk once an hour or ninety minutes and stretch?

Or walk to get some water. How about beginning with a daily five-minute walk? You can build on your successes in the small things.

When I was in Weight Watchers the instructor read a poem from the perspective of a single pound. Nobody wanted to lose just one pound, but three or five or ten. Generally, we don't embrace the small steps. We would do well to remember that all those small steps add up, all those single pounds become three, five or ten pounds.

Consider how we treat our little children. When I watched as my granddaughter started taking her first wobbly steps at thirteen months, we cheered her on. There were other grandparents who said their grandchildren were fully walking around at nine months. Was my granddaughter behind? She's running now! What if we hadn't celebrated her little moments? Instead, we celebrated every step!

In the process of her growth, it illuminated to me how we don't give ourselves the same level of reassurance and praise in the small things. Instead of encouraging ourselves through new beginnings, and setbacks, we beat ourselves up. Even after all this time, I still have to remind myself that I can choose to celebrate all that my body has done for me, and all that it allows me to experience, rather than look at it as the enemy when I can't do what I want to do.

Recently on Instagram, I read something posted by Lexy Florentina. "And then her body whispered, I'm not fighting against you. I'm fighting for you. Through pain and tension, I communicate the boundaries you never learned to set. Through fatigue and exhaustion, I give you the rest you were never allowed to take. Through the headaches and the brain fog, I let you know that you're doing too much. You see, I've always been on your side. I'm just waiting for you to be on mine."

Our body always prioritizes us, but we don't always prioritize our body.

Take the opportunity to see things differently. Give yourself the freedom to look at your priorities and consider different options to fortify yourself as you move about your world.

Importance of Rest

Rest is another one of those things we push aside under pressure. We don't give ourselves rest until our body takes it from us. That happened to me recently. I had a wonderful fun week with friends and was careful not to overdo anything, and we had a great time. While planning a night out to a concert, I prioritized the needs of my body over a look that would have cost me physically as the night wore on. What I remembered about this stadium was how far we'd have to walk to and from our transportation.

With the outfit I was putting together—silver, sparkles, and a western theme—a pair of crystal covered boots would have been the just right amount of embellishment. Yet I opted to wear silver sneakers keeping my look on theme and still cute. Despite the heat, I was cool and comfortable. We had a long way to walk, and when it really mattered, I was glad I'd worn the sneakers.

At the beginning of the night, as we went into the concert, I saw a very attractive woman in a sheer sparkly jumpsuit. She'd spent some time choosing her beautifully coordinated outfit; her hair and makeup were just right. Then I noticed her shoes—which were gorgeous!—but she could barely walk. It was obvious to me her feet were screaming because she was taking little bitty steps. She had no bag with an extra set of shoes. She was in serious pain already.

What we prioritize affects how we show up. I wanted to have fun and be comfortable. The other woman chose to be stunning. I was free to dance if I wanted to or sit if I needed to. I was able to enjoy that concert in a way the other lady probably didn't. Hurting feet can affect your whole night. Had I stubbornly made the choice to prioritize a certain look over my body, I could have been in pain too. That would have prevented me from laughing and enjoying my friends, and noticing the experience of the others around me, all of which I appreciated and enjoyed immensely. What a blast!

Afterward, I walked the mile to the car. I was sweaty and tired as was everyone else in the ninety-five-degree South Florida heat at eleven o'clock at night. But I'm proud of the choice I made early on; because I knew — and brought to my self-awareness — what I would need by the end.

I did well until I got home. Then, I turned right around and hopped in the car for a long drive to see about a family member. The reason I chose to go was important enough to set my needs aside and put my body on the line. I knew the trip would draw from and likely deplete my energy reserves. Because I knew what I could do to restore myself, I went anyway. I prioritized that trip fully aware of the physical cost, with a recovery plan already in place.

Sometimes we prioritize something that will be hard and cost us health wise. I'm not saying you should never do this; sometimes it's necessary like when there's a family emergency or other circumstance of importance. The difference is knowing you're doing it and planning for your aftercare. When you don't realize it, you burn the candle at both ends. Then you wonder why nothing's left for you, why you're stressed and cranky, and why you feel exhausted. If you bring awareness to your situation, you can monitor when a circumstance or choice is too much or might cost more than you want to give. With awareness, you learn to prioritize well-being for yourself and make plans for restorative action.

For Your Consideration

1. When you look over your responsibilities, are you putting yourself on the list?
2. What bedtime and wake up routines are you currently practicing? How can you improve them to set yourself up for a great start each day or a better night's rest?
3. Where are the overlooked parts of your day that you can take mini breaks to breathe or affirm yourself?

8 Perseverance

You don't often have a choice about what life throws at you. There will always be unexpected events to challenge you: The promotion is given to someone else. The sponsorship you hoped and trained for gets pulled, you lose a loved one, or you hear a disappointing health report. Maybe the project is bigger or more involved than first imagined, the job doesn't live up to its promise, or a goal you wanted to reach is taking longer than hoped.

How do you deal with it? You have several choices. One is that you could be temporarily sidelined. You might need to pause for a while and process what is occurring. You may need to grieve, regroup, or develop a strategy to overcome the situation.

A second option is letting it undermine you or become so central to your life that you are unable to move on. The impact on your present and future is stagnating.

The third option is that you can persevere, come through, and grow forward. Perseverance at its core is persisting, enduring, or being dedicated to seeing something through. To keep going when it looks like the odds are not in your favor. It may require digging deep into yourself to find the will to not only finish but finish well. Perseverance may look different for each person and change according to circumstances.

In the Bible, a champion who perseveres gets the crown. James 1:2-4 speaks about considering all trials as joy. Not because those events are joyful, but because they provide opportunity to mature in facets of your faith and character. This isn't a mandate to strap in and smile through your pain as if your ability to do so demonstrates strength. However, when we persevere through our trials, we build endurance, resilience, and wisdom.

When something devastating happens, it isn't easy to make meaning in the moment – nor should that be your goal — but an unexpected circumstance or event can reveal strengths that you didn't know you had. They bring people into your orbit that you might not otherwise have met; people who can encourage, inspire, motivate, and offer a fresh perspective. If you allow it, perseverance can reveal new avenues of maturity and creativity.

Shades of Persistence

In my experience, there are three kinds of perseverance: conscious, reflexive, or subconscious. There will be times when persisting will exhaust you. There may be times that you need to take a break. You may even ponder your options, as in *what happens if I stop persisting?* The choice to continue your path in the face of tragedy is quite often reflexive. You might be blindsided by events and sense you have no choice but to keep moving — processing after you endure. Somehow you get through the situation, doing your best with the resources you have at the time.

Conscious perseverance is planning to see something through to the end, no matter how long it takes. These could be career aspirations, bucket list experiences, educational goals, or health-related outcomes. Conscious perseverance usually involves strategies, parameters and stated outcomes.

Subconscious persistence is similar to reflexive. Sometimes it may be doing the same things hoping for different results but staying the course regardless. It may be pursuing an endeavor that proves fruitless or staying in a damaging relationship. You may be hoping to redeem all the time you've invested in a job or relationship. You may be at a loss as to how to move forward in a different way. There seems to be no clear goal and no lasting forward motion. It may be necessary to talk to someone and see what other options exist and to clarify your goals and desires.

Conscious

Devon has been an elite decathlete for many years. As an NCAA champion, professional athlete, and Olympic hopeful, he is fully aware of his goals. He desires to represent the United States in the next Olympiad. He has the talent, and he's counted the costs. He's doing the hard work of showing up to training day after day, year after year. He competes around the world racking up wins, losses, and lessons.

He's conscious of what and how much he feeds his body, and he trains hard. Devon is no stranger to setbacks. He's searched out the self-care assistance he needed to fight through disappointments and depression. He knows that perseverance is a vital part of success. So, despite injuries—some resulting in surgeries—losing sponsorships, and at times having no track club, Devon persisted in training, at times by himself.

Some might have said, "It's okay. I gave it my best. It's time to move on. It's time to grow up and get a job." And that could have been a fine choice. That would have been the wrong choice for Devon. He chooses to persevere, doggedly pursuing his dream until it's no longer an option. Devon's whole life and focus revolves around this singular pursuit.

As a world-class athlete, Devon is dedicated to this path more than ever. He's making a comeback and moving up in the international space. As I write this, we don't know if he'll achieve his goal of being in the next Summer Olympics. But I am confident that the lessons learned, resilience gained, and the satisfaction of giving his all will set him up for a very bright future.

Reflexive

When I was given my first cancer diagnosis at seventeen, doctors initially said my condition carried about a 20 percent chance of survival. Through what I believe are miraculous circumstances, I had the best medical intervention available and… I got to live! Living a full life forty-two years later with a grandchild is beyond my wildest dream.

At seventeen, I didn't think about persevering,

I just did what I had to do. To me the choice was do it or give up. Though I expected to die, I wasn't going to go out without a fight. I wasn't going to let this tragedy be meaningless. As I went through all the tests and procedures, there were times when I had a sense of purpose. At other times I didn't know anything else to do, so I stayed the course. In moments of weariness, I did entertain the thought, "What if we just let the end happen?" But mostly, I was on autopilot. It was a reflex—not doing it wasn't an option—at least, not one I considered for long.

Being dedicated or persevering does not mean the path will be easy. Probably everyone has had moments of weakness where they considered the cost of giving up. Persisting doesn't keep that feeling from coming, but neither does it allow fear or apathy to swallow you up.

Recently, two of my friends have each lost a child. I can't imagine a loss more devastating. My heart breaks for them. As a therapist, I am also aware that somewhere down the grieving road, these parents will eventually reenvision life and find a way to make meaning from their pain. They'll find a way to keep going for themselves and their loved ones.

In the tragedy and loss space, perseverance can

be tricky. The path through is neither linear nor predictable. Much depends on the individual's capacity for self-awareness, acceptance of the circumstance, and vulnerability. We move forward, we adjust, and we correct our course as needed.

Perseverance and Self-Care

Caring for yourself while persevering requires that you be cognizant of your physical and emotional needs. This includes knowing when something becomes too much, when to take a break, making room to grieve losses, and rebounding when things don't go as planned. There's much to be gained by achieving the goal, surviving the tragedy, enduring the loss while knowing you stayed in it, even when you don't know what's on the other side.

With a goal like becoming an Olympian, you may envision yourself with the medal and the title. In the case of loss, you learn to imagine a good life without that loved one. What does life look like beyond the cancer diagnosis?

The timeline of perseverance is that it takes as long as it takes. You'll have automatic days and conscious days and maybe some unconscious ones. This season will not last forever. I applaud you for taking the necessary steps to care for yourself.

There's no shame in getting the oil changed in your car, vacuuming your carpet, or taking medicine for a cold. Likewise, it's also great self-care to seek wisdom and counsel to get through such a season. If you don't know what to do, or feel you don't have what it takes, it doesn't mean you're deficient. It means you're self-aware and that you need new or better tools to navigate a situation. It's always okay to get the help you need to process grief, heal from trauma, or persist toward a dream. It's advisable to talk to someone about anxiety that feels out of control to you. It's courageous to ask for help. It's not a weakness; it's a power move.

Then one day, you're on the other side. You're the Olympian. You survived the diagnosis. You're a couple years past the loss and you're finding meaning in life. After reaching the other side, there's an opportunity for your spirit to feel fortified. I think about all the experiences that I didn't allow fear or inertia to rob from me. By persisting in pushing through those barriers, I expanded my perception of what is possible for me.

For Your Consideration

1. Where in your history do you have examples of perseverance? How did those times shape you and inform your self-awareness?
2. Is there a time in your life where you have persevered consciously, reflexively, or subconsciously? How are the experiences similar? How are they different?
3. Now that you're aware of the different shades of persistence, how might you apply what you've learned? Would you have done anything differently?

EMOTIONAL

9 Grief and Loss

Many people take pride in their lawns. You may even be part of a friendly lawn competition. You spend all spring and summer dumping chemicals on the weeds or popping flower heads off. But all that does is prevent them from growing above the ground, keeping them from the sun and the water.

By late summer, our lawns are looking good. We believe we've handled the weeds. But actually, we've only popped off the heads and dumped chemicals on top, forcing them to go underground for nourishment. When the conditions are right the next spring, they blow up all over the yard as if you hadn't done anything. These new shoots may appear to be unrelated to last year's plants, but underneath, the roots are connected. What you might find is that every weed doesn't represent an individual plant. It's connected to a system of roots.

You might have a hundred plants, yet ten thousand weeds. This illustrates the cumulative effect of ungrieved losses.

Because we, as a society, don't know all the things we're allowed to mourn, much of what we carry individually are ungrieved or unprocessed losses. These get set aside and eventually get buried under the more pressing concerns of our days. What the mental health field now knows about unprocessed grief and loss is that it doesn't just add on, or even multiply on. It multiplies exponentially. And eventually, it's going to surface.

I experienced this in my late twenties. At the time, I was hundreds of miles away from my siblings and my dad. I remember being incredibly sad about my mother's untimely death and deeply felt the loss. I went through some depression, and it affected a lot in my life.

After she passed, life sped along. Four years later, I was the young mother of two sons, seven and three. My eldest was in second grade at a little Christian school. I picked him up every day, and every day was the same. He raced into the house, dropped his coat and backpack in front of the closet. He ran around, went to the bathroom, then played with his three-year-old brother.

Every day I reminded my oldest, "Come pick

up your coat. Put your backpack where it belongs." He knew he was supposed to do it, but the routine was that he didn't do it until I told him the second time. This day was different.

It was like an out-of-body experience. I saw myself yelling and going off on this little boy. He just stood there, not understanding what he'd done wrong. His little brother stayed out of my way. My boys were terrified, and I was unable to stop myself. Though I never physically touched them, I knew I'd lost control.

The faith community had just started to acknowledge that psychology was not quack science. I'd been listening to a Christian radio program called the *Minerth & Meier Hour*. They always ended the same way. "If you find yourself needing help, call 1-800-NEWLIFE." That number was in my head.

I remember telling my son, "I'm so sorry. Can you get a snack for you and your brother? Mommy has to make a phone call." I went to another room and called the number. And they connected me to my first counselor.

I hadn't been okay for a while. There had been tension in the marriage; I was irritable, depressed, and crying all the time even though nothing bad was happening. I felt disconnected from my husband and my faith, and always felt on edge. I looked forward to finally getting some answers. Several sessions later, after explaining family dynamics, all that I had been feeling and my general coping mechanisms, she confronted me with her conclusion.

"You haven't grieved the loss of your mother."

I was confused. What does that have to do with me yelling at my son? She explained it wasn't the cause, but it's in the soup of things that were repressed. She tied things to the unfinished processing of my mother's death. Outside of that context, I would never have put that together. She helped me understand you could be sad, you could cry, you could miss a person, a thing, a place or what have you, and still not grieve the loss. To me, that was huge! I didn't begin grieving my mother until four years after her death.

Shortly after my mom died, my older brother said to me, "How does it feel to be the leader of the grief process?" I felt like he'd given me an assignment, and I took that on. I thought, "Oh! Well, now I know what to do." By taking care of everybody else, I outsourced my grief. I'd gone back to Chicago after my mother's funeral and laid on the couch for a few months, drank milk and ate cookies, and gained twenty pounds. I got pregnant with my second child and continued looking after everybody else out of a sense of responsibility. I poured out without supporting myself. Until other areas of my life blew up or stopped functioning, I thought I was fine.

All I had really done was "pop the heads off the weeds," depriving grief of water and light. Instead of going away, those losses went underground. After this event, I became aware of my tendency to take care of others and overcommit at my expense. Now I'm better able to catch that tendency before heavy costs are incurred.

Ungrieved Losses Affect Relationships

As a clinician, I've learned that even though grief is a universal experience, we typically don't know how to process it. If someone dies, we know what to do. There's a ceremony to attend. We take food to the family, we offer condolences, and we send flowers or cards. We know what to do. Not so with losses that we don't acknowledge.

Unprocessed grief and loss have the potential to affect everything. It can profoundly impact relationships. A person wanting to avoid or bypass processing their grief and loss will probably outsource their emotional work to something else. What matters is *why* you are doing it. Are you nurturing or numbing? Are you working toward getting in touch with your emotions or preventing them from emerging?

An example might be to distract with exercise or body building, excessive work, or travel. These are healthy-looking avenues of emotion regulation that will reap positive benefits on one level. You may look great physically, bring home fatter paychecks, or enjoy wonderfully fun experiences in Cabo or Greece. But those have not addressed the grief or loss. If you distract yourself instead of processing or acknowledging your emotions, you still harbor unprocessed grief and loss. This will express itself at some unpredictable future point.

Equally concerning, but potentially more damaging, is how you choose to regulate your emotions; especially with something that carries its own problems, such as drugs, alcohol, under- or overeating, or cutting. When so much is going on in a person's head, this second set of emotion regulators silences the noise temporarily. It might feel good at first. It may feel as though it works because it does bring temporary relief. However, the more often these dysfunctional behaviors are engaged, the more noticeable and entrenched they become. They carry consequences of their own.

One adage explains it like this: the man takes the drug, the drug takes the drug, then the drug takes the man. That is to say, whatever a person runs to—be it the unhealthy relationship or the drug—that distraction can become its own trap. And now, you not only have the first problem you are avoiding, but now you have a new set of problems.

In both cases, the source is the same. Without addressing the real underlying problem, emotion regulators provide a false sense of control. However, you can't regulate emotions you don't acknowledge. Dealing with the source head-on prevents additional unwanted problems later.

Anniversaries, Guilt, and Growth

Before the realization that I hadn't fully grieved the loss of my mother, the days around the anniversary of her death I was moody and irritable and definitely carb loading. By the time she'd been gone seven or eight years, I had fully grieved and accepted the loss. The anniversaries didn't always affect me the same way.

Keeping the anniversary of a death or significant events is a natural part of our time-tracking design. Our culture celebrates the annual remembrance of big moments. Losing a loved one is significant. It's possible to get caught up in how we're "supposed" to react on those days. For the first several years you may feel as emotional as you did on the day it occurred. Over time, our mind adjusts to the loss, and it isn't felt as sharply.

In looking at a calendar one year, I noticed the date of my mother's death had passed and I'd missed it. The first time it happened, I struggled with a lot of guilt—a sense that I was forgetting her. Was this a reflection of my love for her? How could I forget?

If you miss or move past an anniversary, it's common to feel a sense of guilt; feel free to not judge yourself. It's going to happen sooner or later, and it's healthy. It means you're not tied to that grief in a way that prevents you from moving through and living your life.

How should we note anniversaries or other devastating events? We give death so much attention, but we're uncertain how to normalize the annual remembrance. If a loss is overwhelming, let it be overwhelming until it isn't. You may feel the loss of someone or something acutely for several years.

That's typical because you're working through it.

The entire year following the death of a loved one is difficult because you're experiencing your special shared events, like first spring planting or ball games or holidays, without them. We have no grid for what that's supposed to look like. If you find yourself recalling painful anniversaries of other kinds of loss, the mechanism is the same. Feel the feelings, name the feelings, give yourself grace over judgment and move through it.

It's common in our current society to hear, "Get over it." You don't have to accept that from anyone. If we "get over" a loss, leaping over it in an effort to avoid the pain instead of going through it, we miss some things. That ungrieved loss remains. When you go *through* it, acceptance, appreciation, and meaning-making can emerge.

I love the verse in II Corinthians 10 about taking every thought captive. Some believe that means grab that thought and don't think that thought! Or they want to grab it and throw it away! But historically, you take captives and set them aside where they can't harm the rest of the population. You keep them alive while you interrogate them and get the information you need. In cognitive behavioral therapy (CBT), we pull them out, look at them and deconstruct them. Analyze your thoughts, study the layers and levels and different applications to understand them. Take what you can use and discard the rest. You might acknowledge the differences from one year to the next. How are you different? How have you changed?

Acknowledging anniversaries is part of healthy processing. It takes time and is different for everyone. Occasionally, you may be triggered. At times I've acknowledged the anniversary of a death or a painful event, yet my life didn't stop. The anniversaries eventually become points of reference. They aren't always a big moment.

One day you will no longer live through the bottleneck of the dates of those anniversaries. You aren't reliving it every year; you're remembering. Lessons were learned, blind spots revealed, and a lot of growth took place. By doing the work of grieving, those anniversaries will no longer have the power to derail you. You'll have the freedom to live your life embracing the places in your life where that person or event influenced you.

Some people get stuck on anniversaries and caught up in memorializing, which can prevent you from moving on. Maybe there's a part of you that's afraid to let go. Regarding the loss of a person, maybe you're concerned that you'll forget how much they meant to you. It honors the person you lost when you see the whole individual. If it's the loss of a relationship, possibly you haven't finished learning the life lessons it contains. You honor the loss of a relationship by acknowledging the aspects of it that brought you together. It also honors who you were at that time. Recognize that anniversaries of events will be part of your life. Although that significant event happened on a day, the event itself isn't reoccurring every year. That event doesn't define your future. It doesn't have to ruin your day. You don't have to give them center stage every year. Nor should you feel bad when you don't.

Dealing with Grief and Loss

I'm often asked, "How do I know if I've fully processed a loss? What if I'm not sure I've grieved the loss? How do I know if I'm doing it right? What does it look like?"

A benchmark I've used regarding the loss of a person of significance is asking, "How do you see them now? Do you see the complete individual?" For a long time, I only saw the best things about my mother. She was cool, available, wise, fashionable, and fun. She was a truth teller and when she spoke, you believed her. But she could also be manipulative and struggled with some self-defeating habits.

That also is my mom, whom I miss and love. I realized how much grief work I had done when I finally saw her as a whole woman. Only then was I able to lay that person to rest.

Maybe you still see them as your "dear sainted" parent or your "dear sainted" grandmother, and all you talk about and remember is dear sainted. Or it could be the opposite, "I'm glad that bum is gone! He was only this, or she was only that." Although it's the opposite side of the same coin, it's still a one-sided, unbalanced perspective. We're all multidimensional. No one is "always" and "never" anything. When you think of them, do you see the entire individual? The good and the bad? Their beauty and their flaws? Their gifts and limitations? If not, you may have some unfinished grief to work through. I've found a "loss line" can be a great tool. A loss line can also include regrets, or those expectations that never came to be.

A loss line is a powerful intervention I do with clients. Your loss line can be a timeline, a chart, or bullet points of your losses from early childhood to present. However you choose to represent it is fine. Events that seem small now may have been monumental at the time. All of us have buried a lot of things. Once you begin thinking about it, more memories will come to mind. When they surface, write them down. Go back and put them in chronological order.

Even things like: My best friend moved away when I was six. We promised to write every day, but we never did. I lost my dog. Or my very first pet—a goldfish—died and was flushed down the toilet. We said goodbye, but that was it. If nobody helped you process the loss of something you cared for or cared about, that's an ungrieved loss.

If you moved, you might have lost your childhood home, your best friends, teachers, and cherished neighbors. Some things you may not have known how to grieve. You might have thought, "That's life," and tossed them aside. Although that loss may have been significant to you, it gets added to all the other unprocessed losses. All those things add up. They go underground and you give them no light. At some future time, when conditions are right, they will pop up in your life, just like that yard full of weeds in spring.

As you remember and talk about those things and ask questions, some losses will be sharp. You can safely acknowledge, "Wow, that hurt!" Others may feel less important, but you get to consider how you feel about them; and when to say, "Okay, I can move on." When you're finished, you might feel the weight of those losses that you thought were no big deal. You might choose to give a collective honoring and burying of what you lost. Or you might decide certain ones deserve a ceremony of sorts.

A former client had come to me completely devastated by the breakup of a long-term relationship with lots of expectations. What do you do with that hurt? Eat a pint of ice cream? That's what movies tell you to do. Hallmark might have a card for it now. But based on this grief and loss concept, the client and I discussed how to lay this relationship and the attached grief and loss to rest.

She shared this concept with her sisters, and they took it from there. She thought they had invited her out for a family dinner. But they had arranged a surprise "Dearly Departed John" funeral, replete with words spoken over the "deceased," and a cake made in his likeness lying in a casket. They acknowledged her loss, and they supported her. It was validating. It was hilarious. They made fun of it. It was an over-the-top gesture, but it offered the closure she needed to move forward.

Every loss doesn't need its own big moment. But choosing to honor and process each remembered loss in your own way is freeing.

For Your Consideration

1) What do you notice about yourself around your loss-related anniversaries?
2) Do you have a balanced view of the individual you lost?
3) Create a loss line by going back to your earliest memories. Write whatever you remember about the things that hurt you. They can be big or small. Think about those things in your past that never had a chance to be acknowledged. What events never had an opportunity to be seen or felt or acknowledged? Then put them in chronological order.

10 Happiness and Joy

What makes each person happy can be as varied as the people you ask. It's interesting to note that even the writers of the US Declaration of Independence included *the right to pursue happiness.* Their insightful choice of words seems to suggest that whatever makes us happy in this moment may not last into the next. But that we have the right to pursue the next thing as well, for as long as we live.

I've come to realize that happiness is slippery, hard to hold onto, and is largely circumstantial. You can have circumstances that please you, that you enjoy, and that you are content with. Let's say for example, a cruise. But if the cruise ship runs aground, has technical difficulties that affect its passengers, or runs into a storm at sea, your happiness could evaporate within seconds. Even if all goes well on your cruise, once you return home, there will be different circumstances that can affect your level of happiness. Happiness and sadness are two opposite ends of the continuum. Sadness too is circumstantial.

A related word is joy. Joy is internal. Joy and hope are at one end of a continuum while despair and hopelessness are at the other. Just as circumstances are the source of happiness, joy also has a source. Joy comes from the soul, which is fed by something or someone. For me, that someone is God. For others it could be fed by their values and principles. Although you can feel joy and happiness, joy differs from happiness in that it abides in your soul. It may surprise you to know that you can feel sadness and joy at the same time. My soul is the reservoir of my joy, peace, and hope.

Today, I may feel somewhat depleted from traveling, very sad because of circumstances, and physically, I may not feel well. Yet, I still have joy. I can be sad for my two friends who have experienced the loss of loved ones, for the woman I know going through a very difficult marriage, and about the damaging behaviors I see from people I care about, but I am not depressed.

Someone may say I'm depressed, when really they're just very sad. Sadness is experiential and circumstance related, whereas depression is a soul (mind, will, emotions and body) condition. One can endure an incredible loss and feel extreme sadness, yet not be in hopeless despair.

Happiness Snare

Where I see people shortchanging themselves is by only pursuing happiness. Because happiness is fleeting, I can be happy today and sad tomorrow. I can be happy that I look good and got lots of compliments, or that the checkbook is on the plus side, which is wonderful. However, I can have joy whether someone affirms me or not, whether I have a lot of money in the bank account or none at all.

Have you ever known someone who had so little, but despite that seemed so joyful? They had very few creature comforts, but they were grounded and steady and emanated peace, joy, and hopefulness? They've figured out how to transcend their circumstances.

A person whose house burns to the ground may be extremely sad that they lost all their belongings, but joyful that all of their family survived. That's the person who has taken care of themselves and their soul. They already know what some of us are still learning and we cannot always control our situations. And their joy doesn't depend on being able to.

Looking for Heaven

Our culture pushes us to pursue happiness. There is nothing inherently wrong with that; as stated earlier, it's a valid pursuit and our birthright. I love the phrase, "We're spiritual beings having an earthly experience." My husband has often said, "You know, this isn't Heaven." But how many of us spin our wheels trying to have all the things that we think will make us happy, while seeking after pleasure and fulfillment and thrills? We spend much of our lives trying to remove ourselves from the experience of pain, seeking distractions, or searching for perfect community. We think pursuing those things will make us happy. And maybe for a while, they do. But how long does it last?

Most of us have learned from experience that even when we obtain any or all of those things, it isn't long before we're looking at the next thing. In a way, we are looking for Heaven's happiness here on earth. We do ourselves a great service when we leave room for both truths — happiness derived from circumstances and joy fed from a reservoir of the soul. We can absolutely live an abundant life, filled with the elements, qualities, and experiences we desire and design.

Fleeting Happiness

For those pursuing self-care I encourage you to recognize when you're pursuing that which is fleeting and circumstantial. I'm not saying you can't have happiness. To some extent, happiness and its pursuit is essential but not sufficient. We all need a joy that feeds our soul, not just our mood. Happiness in and of itself is not fulfilling; it will deplete you in the long run.

For example, I really enjoy my cup of coffee in the morning. I almost feel like I can't journal my gratitudes and spend time with the Lord without it; it's a significant part of how I set up my day. Those first few sips are just so satisfying when the temperature is just right. But if coffee is all I have, it will deplete me. I really don't get nutrition from it, so I can't just drink coffee all day, every day and be truly happy. I know that coffee isn't going to sustain me in the long term.

If I don't also drink water and have breakfast, or receive the things that nourish my body, mind, soul, and emotions, it's not going to matter that I sat down and had a happy experience with a cup of coffee. It is imperative to find a way to feed your inner person. Since this isn't Heaven, we won't live a pain-free existence here; it's only painless there. We shortchange our definitions of what abundance is by always tying it to physical and fleeting things.

Currently, much of the self-care culture revolves around the pursuit of beautification, massages, and vacations, or that which removes you from all the things about your life that are uncomfortable. I say, do all those things that help fortify your body and reduce cortisol levels. Spend time in the company of people who make you laugh or read books that touch your emotions. Do all of those things. But if you're not also caring for your inner person, the core of you, you'll be running like a hamster on a wheel choosing the next distraction.

All the topics in this book address you facet by facet for the benefit of the integrated whole. You are a collective, connected being. Feed your soul by engaging those things that seem difficult.

An examined life feeds your joy. When you can face your life, no matter what is happening in it, and find joy in each moment, you will be connected to something far beyond happiness. When you can be content with much or little and see beyond your physical existence to your spiritual one, you will have found joy. When you can be hopeful in the midst of tough circumstances in spite of the evidence, you will feel a deep sense of gratitude. In the transcendent moment that you realize you're experiencing joy and sadness at the same time, you'll see how they can coexist simultaneously. You will have learned what really matters and found the source of what feeds your soul.

For Your Consideration

1. What are those things for you that feed your inner person? In the recent past, what would you have said makes you happy?
2. As you care for yourself, what might you do differently to nurture your soul?
3. Today, which are you most in touch with, your joy or your happiness? What steps can you take to go deeper?

RELATIONAL

11 Friendship

Almost everyone has a close trusted friend that they swear to secrecy. And you might have evaluated a friend's loyalty by how well they kept your confidences. Friends are not only repositories of your confidence, but they're as complex and multifaceted as we are. Understanding the nature of your friendships and nurturing their place in your life is essential to well-being. Your friendships play an important role in meeting your core longings, particularly for security, belonging, and significance.

In recent years, much emphasis has been placed on spouses or romantic partners being the "best friend." Our grandparents certainly didn't use best friend status as a foundation for marriage.

Loving and marrying your best friend seems more like a Hollywood construct. Though friendship is an important element of romantic partnership or marriage, the concept of marrying your best friend suggests that your marriage partner should be all things all the time. This puts enormous pressure on the spouse. If you were to have a marital concern with "your best friend," to whom would you go for counsel?

It's been said that friends are the family you choose. They hold a special place in our hearts for good reason. They are close enough to understand how we feel and can be objective without being judgmental. Friend relationships have immeasurable impact on our lives. How do friendships nurture your soul?

Birds of a Feather

We are drawn to people based on common experiences, shared interests, lifestyle, or perspective. There is generally some mutual understanding and thus validation of each other's experience. Friends satisfy a core longing to be accepted, known, and understood. They are an essential element of community, and we're wired for it.

As we mature, we recognize that each relationship will be different. Because we have many facets of personality, one friend cannot be all things to us. There are those who can only celebrate with you, some who will only grieve with you. Fair weather friends, and foul weather friends, see you once-a-year friends, and of course—the one who knows where the proverbial bodies are buried. Each of them shares something with you that others do not and brings something to your life the others can't. These connections should be mutual and reciprocal.

I visualize friendships as concentric circles around the individual. Each ring represents a differing level of intimacy, access, and trust. Not everybody will be, nor can be, in your close inner circle. There are those that will be right next to your heart, very close to the chest. Those bosom buddies can share your dreams and disappointments and walk along with you. Conversely, because friendships serve different purposes, you don't have to dismiss someone who's positioned in one of your outer circles. These acquaintance relationships are also valuable: you can appreciate them for what they are.

Let's explore a few important attributes of friendship that boost self-care.

Friend-View Mirror

We've talked about having trusted people who can speak truth into our lives especially regarding our blind areas. These same people help reign us in when we're going off course. Friends can get away with saying things that we may not hear from a parent, sibling, or spouse. They often see what we cannot.

My husband and I have talked at length defining what support really means to each of us. We sometimes miss the ways we best to support each other. For instance, he knows I have an old (largely unsubstantiated) narrative around the feeling he doesn't support me in certain ways. My inner circle girlfriends also know this, and they challenge me. At an event in the recent past, my husband publicly expressed very thoughtful and kind things about me in a room filled with loved ones, friends, and colleagues. But my narrative kicked in, and I almost missed it. My girlfriends took that opportunity to speak into my life. "Davia, we've been around and have seen your dynamic. Pay attention. We all know he means it."

Because these women have trusted access to my vulnerable spaces and have demonstrated honesty and trustworthiness time and again, I know they speak from a place of love. They have the authority to challenge me — and I receive it.

Friends love us right where we are. When connecting with them, there are no preconditions. They don't tell us, "If you get yourself straight, I'll be your friend." Close friends love you right where you are — but they care enough to not leave you there. Dear friends tell you the truth about who you are and remind you of the good they see in you. When I'm going through challenges, they tell me things I may not want to hear but that are nonetheless true. I can take their words to heart and become a better version of myself, and a better friend to them.

When friends truly want our best, they can offer unique perspectives on our blind areas. They can share valuable insight into who we are and how we show up in life. Understanding your value as a person and as a friend to someone else is self-care.

We need to know we are loved and appreciated and that we matter to someone. It feeds a purpose in us to be accepted. Friends encourage us with their kind words and observations and validate us and our experiences.

At a dear friend's milestone birthday party, each guest received a beautiful, handcrafted card made specifically for that individual. Every card was different and personalized even further with a message inside. My friend wanted each of us to know why we were invited. We stood up one by one to read in her words what each of us meant to her. That incredible gesture let us know, *you all are my inner people*! There wasn't a dry eye in the place. It was brilliant, humbling, and masterfully done.

It just affirmed the importance of friendship. There's something about feeling safety in a non-judgmental space and being with those who really want your best and to see you reach your full potential. Friends are willing to cheer you on but also get in the trenches with you. When they see you acting contrary to the way you say you are, they'll call you on it and they'll stay with you until you're back on track. That's important. Having and enjoying truthful, loving friendship is self-care.

Friends Encourage

I saw my dear friend Steve at a reunion party this year. He's a media person, an established presence in a large market. Steve is Mr. Social, a delightful person, our go-to planning committee. Everybody wants to see him and have a chance to talk with him. But this time, he made a point to take me aside for a little serious conversation.

"I have to tell you that I watch everything that you do. And you have a gift Davia," he said. "You have a way of bringing a person in, in a short period of time. When I look at even your two-minute Instagram posts, I feel like you're talking to me. That's a gift."

I've known Steve for over forty years. His comment was so encouraging! Not only because he's highly accomplished in his field, but because he was so intentional in letting me know that he'd been paying attention.

"I'm just waiting," he said. "Somebody's going to find you. Keep putting it out there. You're bigger than this. I'm so proud of you!"

One of the most wonderful gifts about friends is that they don't see us through our eyes; they're not limited by our personal vision. And it can be very uplifting to see yourself through theirs.

Reflections of Ourselves

There's a lot you learn about yourself in your friendships. I had to learn when to bring people in. Initially, I didn't wait until you proved something, nor had we come to any kind of common experience. We were just in the same place together: school, college, or worship. I would just bring you in first as my friend. Over time, I learned to assess what solid friendships are made of and the kinds of people I wanted to be friends with.

Right now, I have incredible friendships; many I've had forever. My childhood friends and I have a shared history, and we talk about how unique our experience is. There aren't many people who maintain deep friendships from grade school, but we have remained engaged in each other's lives for decades.

My current circle of girlfriends didn't need all that time to go deep. We believe God placed us in one another's lives. Although we have the same faith, we don't worship together. We're from different generations, but we offer each other a haven that is unbelievable.

In fact, one of them introduced me to one of her people. "You two are so similar, and you play a similar role in my life. I don't feel like I have what either of you need, but you each have what the other needs. I think you need each other in a way I can't be available for you. I want to get you together." She'd been dropping this seed for some time and finally arranged a meeting. The three of us had cocktails, and we just leaned in.

What a humble position to take. In this group

of women, there's a strong sense of absolute acceptance and celebration of who you are. There's no jealousy, and no hidden agenda.

We check in with each other so there's a level of accountability. When one of us has a situation that isn't working, there's a challenge. When there's sorrow or loss, we lean in and support. These are my friends. We lead with our strengths and rest in our safety.

Lost or Broken

We often enter friendships hoping they will last always. But even our most cherished friendships may not be forever. Sometimes under the most positive circumstances, with no disagreement or falling out, a friendship can drift apart. Maybe life naturally took you in different directions. Maybe your priorities and interests changed, or a relocation disrupted the flow of your interactions. Maybe your season with that person has ended. For many, losing a friendship, especially one that spans years, can be as devastating as a romantic partner breakup.

Some friendships may repeat patterns from your family of origin that keep you in places that are toxic for you. For example, let's say you came from a family that exhibited biting sarcasm or patterns of stonewalling that were painful. A friendship that reflects those same traits may have some initial subconscious attraction due to familiarity. However, as you heal from that pain, you may need to extract yourself from those relationships that no longer align with the healthier you.

Then there are those painful circumstances when a friendship takes a wrong turn. A critical misunderstanding occurs, a broken confidence, or a betrayal. Wondering what happened and how it can be addressed is stressful to say the least. Your expectation may be that if you ever unwittingly hurt or offended your friend, that they would let you know immediately. But navigating a repair is layered and takes time, intention, and humility. It doesn't always happen.

It's possible to bridge these gaps by checking in with a simple question. "Are we okay?" This puts us in a vulnerable position. We take the risk of being hurt by that friend's words or discovering that they've been building a case against us for a long time. A true friend will usually answer honestly. What if the answer is no? As part of caring for yourself, you must decide if the relationship is worthy of your time and capable of repair.

For the moment, let's presume it is. If your friend replies that you're not okay, you have several choices. You can choose to have the difficult conversation — if they allow it. Even in disagreement it's important to respect personal boundaries regardless of where you believe the fault lies.

It's important to be aware of the reality that you may not be the best friend of your best friend. And you may not be the confidant of the person you confide in. You may learn the person you thought of as a close friend isn't able to reciprocate. You may choose to move them to another tier, or to end the friendship.

The internal choice to move a friend to another tier allows you time to consider whether this is the space that brings the most freedom and peace. It gives you the space to thoughtfully consider how to move forward and can sometimes deepen the friendship. Another option is maintaining a valuable relationship as acquaintances rather than intimates. Not every broken relationship can or will be restored. An important part of self-care is understanding and accepting that friendships change—allowing them to be what they are.

Intimate Friends

Intimacy is not the sole purview of romantic relationships, but an essential element of platonic friendship. I love that phrase, into-me-see. Intimacy encompasses familiarity, closeness, understanding, confidence, and caring. I think the more intimate relationships are non-romantic. With friends you operate within the parameters of what-you-see-is-what-you-get, and you're much more open.

As you become more self-aware, you'll be better able to receive people in context. Self-awareness allows you to free people to be who they are. Some friends are happy to lead, guide or listen to your trials or secrets. But some won't be and that's okay. You can be a better friend by freeing them to be themselves, and not requiring of them what they cannot deliver.

You may have a particular friend who is close to your heart. But let's say over time, you sense something is off. Maybe some unhealthy competition or envy has entered the picture and interrupted intimacy. You can still consider them to be very dear, and refer to each other as Aces or Besties, but you know it's become risky to share certain things with them. You may need to quietly adjust that friendship to another tier.

It might look like being less available or guarding your conversations to keep their jealousy at bay. You might reserve discussing your dreams with the people who get excited about them and want to brainstorm with you about how to accomplish them. Elevated self-care means guarding that which is precious to you and nurturing yourself and your relationships while maintaining the best aspects of various concentric circles of friendship. All friends don't have to be all things. Who and what they are is still valuable.

You may have heard that friends come to us for a reason, for a season, or for a lifetime. That phrase is actually the title a poem about friendship. It's a gentle reminder that there is purpose behind each friendship no matter how long they last.

Reason, Season, Lifetime

People come into your life for a reason, a season, or a lifetime.
When you figure out which one it is,
you will know what to do for each person.

When someone is in your life for a REASON, it is usually to meet a need you have expressed.
They have come to assist you through a difficulty;
to provide you with guidance and support;
to aid you physically, emotionally, or spiritually.

They may seem like a godsend, and they are.
They are there for the reason you need them to be.
Then, without any wrongdoing on your part or at an inconvenient time,
this person will say or do something to bring the relationship to an end.

Sometimes they die. Sometimes they walk away.
Sometimes they act up and force you to take a stand.
We must realize that our need has been met, our desire fulfilled; their work is done.

The prayer you sent up has been answered and now it is time to move on.

Some people come into your life for a SEASON, because your turn has come to share, grow, or learn. They bring you an experience of peace or make you laugh.
They may teach you something you have never done. They usually give you an unbelievable amount of joy.
Believe it. It is real. But only for a season.

LIFETIME relationships teach you lifetime lessons; things you must build upon in order to have a solid emotional foundation.
Your job is to accept the lesson, love the person, and put what you have learned to use in all other relationships and areas of your life.
It is said that love is blind, but friendship is clairvoyant.

— Unknown

For Your Consideration

1. Since every friend cannot be all things, do you have an appreciation for what each friend provides? What do they receive from you?

2. Who do you trust with your dreams, fears, concerns? Are you trustworthy?

3. Seeing through the lens of concentric circles, which of your friendships might need to be adjusted closer to or further out?

4. If you've experienced the pain of a broken friendship, how have you repaired or grieved the loss?

12 Conflict

The word conflict is used to describe everything from international war to interpersonal struggles, so let's look at the definition from *Merriam-Webster*. Conflict is defined as: "struggle; clash of interests; opposing polar opinions; it can be protracted; it can be interpersonal within oneself, amongst classes, intrapersonal or relational. Discord, contention, strife, and variance. Disagreement about goals, the path you take, or standards and values." For the purposes of self-care, we'll focus on intrapersonal, interpersonal, and relational.

When two people are in a relationship, at some point they'll come to a crossroads or conflict. The number of things that two people can disagree on is limitless. Between parents and children there could be conflict over education, friends, which college to attend, the quality of spouses-to-be or which career path to take. Conflict between friends could be as lighthearted as which music is best, or as serious as loyalty issues. Between bosses or coworkers, conflict could be about showing up on time, completing responsibilities, and giving respect. Between spouses, conflict may represent opposing views on how to parent, where to worship, how money is spent, and the company each one keeps.

But the inability to agree doesn't mean that a battle must ensue, or as I like to say, conflict doesn't have to mean combat. Our perspective on conflict itself can deeply affect our self-care.

Before I cover some helpful tools, it's important to begin with the knowledge that conflict is reasonable, normal, healthy, and inevitable. It is not a thing to be feared. Because conflict is normal and healthy, we should plan for it. With that in mind, begin collecting tools that will help you turn conflict into a relationship-building asset. Treat conflict as an opportunity to learn more about the person you're in conflict with and to dig into yourself and discover what matters to you and why. What motivates your actions and choices? By uncovering what drives you, you see the conflict in a new light.

Context is paramount, and I'll cover it in more detail in this chapter.

Conflict Effects

Ruminating over serious disagreements can and often does take more attention and mental energy than resolving the issue. You may become stuck in a thought loop, replaying the conflict highlights, which keeps certain emotions engaged. As this overtakes the mental landscape, tensions rise between you and those with whom you disagree. The longer the clash continues, the more time erodes strength and satisfaction from that relationship. Left unresolved, these tugs-of-war can cause wounding or even physical illness. Learning to use tools that help mitigate or resolve conflict is self-care.

You may not always know the best ways to resolve conflict. But you do know that communicating well is one of the most important tools for navigating disagreements. When two people connect with the intent of resolving to maintain the relationship, they can focus on workable solutions that allow both sides to reach an agreement. It's different than confronting "to win" an argument. It isn't bullying another person into submission so one person can have their way. If both people don't win, it's not a win.

When we have a conflict, it usually emanates from a core need, like belonging, safety or significance. When you have a disagreement with your coworker or your boss, often what's really underneath is that you don't feel seen or feel insignificant in that space.

What this means is going back to basics, and relearning how to speak to one another. New communication models require being clear in representing your needs, desires, and expectations. It includes providing missing context, asking questions for understanding, and using "I" statements. Good communication also requires keen listening. I usually start by telling people that learning new patterns of communication seems very elementary and even condescending. Insulting one's intelligence is not the intention, but you must ask yourself, "Is what you're doing really working?"

Think back to when you began learning to read. First you learned the letters. Then wrote them out, which led to writing and reading small words, then short sentences, then paragraphs led to pages and finally entire books.

It's okay to feel elementary, even if it feels a bit contrived — and it is. But that will soon be forgotten when you see positive results. The goal is to take you out of stale, familiar patterns by providing a new template that works. These tools work not only in your closest, most intimate relationships, but in all relationships.

Plan to Succeed

With an eye on resolving conflict, you can set the stage for difficult conversations with ground rules. A certain issue may be pressing on your mind that requires discussion with your spouse, but it never seems to be the right time, whether it's because you're having such a great day, or because they just came home grumpy from work. If you agonize about the appropriate time to bring up a difficult subject, consider taking the temperature of the room. Let's look at an example of how it works.

Let's say the person you need to talk with had a tough day at the office: that's probably not going to be a good time to bring up a deep topic. If they've just gotten home and feel exhausted, depressed, or upset, they may not even be in a place to receive good news, let alone an important conversation. They will likely feel ambushed and become defensive because they're not in the right frame of mind.

Conversations might also be delayed for other

reasons. HHALTBADD is an acronym that reminds us not to have important conversations when at least one of you is hungry, in a hurry, angry, lonely, tired, bored, anxious, drinking or depressed.

Instead, wisely choose the time to ask, "When would be a good time in the next twenty-four hours to discuss concern XYZ?" You can give them a little more latitude by asking your partner [boss, coworker, friend, or whomever] the same question a little differently. "Can you let me know in the next twenty-four hours when is a good time to talk about this?" Now you've allowed them time to consider the issue and prepare for conversation.

A tool that I have often share with my clients is to evaluate how much capacity you have on a scale of 1-10. It's your signal to one another what you're able to handle. For instance, if one of you is at a four, then you'll know not to approach with something deep. Anything below a five usually indicates a level of depletion. Sometimes the person having a better day will share their number. "Well, I'm at an eight, can I help?"

The option to decline and or reschedule is always on the table. If they decline, it's best to graciously provide the space they need. Having been apart all day, there is undoubtedly context you don't have that would explain their mood. Giving a lower number could also signal not being ready to share information about the day. You will still have the opportunity to engage—just not in that moment

Use the Ladder

In the interim, prepare for your conversation with a clear idea of what you want to say, what your concerns are, and the outcomes you hope for. This will help you reach solutions more readily. A helpful tool I often refer to before approaching an important topic is called the Ladder of Integrity. This ladder contains a series of questions developed by Peter and Geri Scazzero authors of the book, *Emotionally Healthy Relationships*.

These questions help you resolve internal conflict by processing each one and writing out your answers. Sometimes, the conflict isn't about another person at all. It clarifies in your own mind why an issue is important, and how you feel about it. It outlines what resolution looks like from your perspective. When both people use this tool, it fosters understanding.

THE LADDER OF INTEGRITY

*DEVELOPED BY PETER &GERI SCAZZERO,
EMOTIONALLY HEALTHY DISCIPLESHIP*

1. Right now the issue on my mind is...
   (I'm anxious in talking about this because...)

2. My part in this is...

3. My need in this issue is...

4. My feelings about this are...
   (What my reaction tells me about me is...)

5. This issue is important to me because I value...
   and I violate that value when...

6. I am willing/not willing to...

7. One thing I could do to improve the situation is...

8. The most important thing I want you to know is...

9. I think my honest sharing will benefit our relationship by...

10. I hope and look forward to...

WHAT IS GOING ON INSIDE ME (1-4), WHAT I VALUE (5-8), WHAT I HOPE (9-10)

These scripts provide a personal framework for gaining clarity about an issue that is on your mind. It may secondarily be used as a communication tool to express yourself honestly while also being respectful and clear about your needs and expectations.

The clarity obtained from these questions will assist in setting you up for constructive dialog and help you move from point to point. I recommend that if you have a hard time discussing difficult topics, use the following questions as a template:

Mind Reading

It is impossible for you to read somebody else's mind. It is disrespectful to assume you know what another person is thinking. Ask permission before you read their mind! This is a simple tool I've used many times in couple's sessions (also from the Scazzeros). When one partner makes a statement starting with "You think," I encourage them to verify. "How do you know that's what they think? Ask permission before you read their mind."

Individuals often respond to what they think somebody else is thinking and develop a whole reaction based their self-derived conclusion. This is not helpful because we are more than likely very far from the truth. And the truth is, we don't know what anybody thinks *unless they tell us*. We're not a two-headed monster. We do not live in another person's head space. Let me illustrate with my favorite *context is everything* story.

I went to one of my son's football games. It was

the last game of the season and their senior day, which meant most of the seniors were playing. The home team crowd was big, compared to the number of fans representing my son's college.

I sat on the end talking with two guys. The picture of us could not have been more different. My look was urban, theirs was rural. I had all kinds of preconceptions about me being the last person they'd want to talk to, but I had a great time chatting with these two men.

I noticed a group of ten to fifteen people, a little way from us. They all wore the same custom t-shirt. And. They. Were. Annoying! They never sat down. They never shut up. All the stuff they were yelling didn't seem to be in concert with the game. I presumed that they were all drunk, though some of them were.

But then I started asking questions. "Who are those people?" I learned the story of one young man on the field. It was his last game. He was nobody's star. He's probably not playing past college. The previous week at a game, this young man's father had a heart attack and died. They buried him the day before this game. These rebel rousers were family and friends being present for that young man. They were in effect saying, "We are here for you. You're gonna hear us no matter where you are.

Whether you're on the bench or on the field. Everybody's going to know that we're here for you."

Did their behavior change? Not at all. But my understanding changed. I went from thinking they were jerks and rebel rousers to being beautiful friends. Even though they never sat and were constantly yelling out their encouragements, I had a more complete picture. Now I understood the context. Context is everything.

We go about each day reacting to people without knowing their experiences. There's a whole life that led up to this moment. In the moment that you interact with someone, are you going to make a judgment about who they are and what they think? You haven't lived their life. You don't even have present context let alone historical context. So instead of jumping to conclusions and reading their mind, you need to ask some questions.

Language Barriers

Since Gary Chapman's book *The Five Love Languages* came on the scene, it has become the go-to for template to understand how to give and receive love in a manner that hits the target. Considering how another person best receives information and trying to deliver it in that manner can go a long way toward each party feeling seen and heard. Keep in mind that your loved ones will naturally speak *their own* love language to you. They may never speak your love language with nuance and fluency; they will speak it with an accent. Give them credit for speaking in a tongue that isn't theirs!

When I've traveled to Spanish-speaking countries, I can ask basic directions and understand conversations if they speak slowly. But let me get lost and the little that I did know disappears from my mind. I can't remember how to ask directions and get frustrated with conjugation. However, I've found repeatedly, any time I try, the person is patient with me. The attempt to speak their language displays a level of respect. When we're under pressure or things get tense, we usually default to speaking our own love language. You may find you also can't think of basic actions to express thoughts in a love language not your own.

One Mother's Day, I woke up filled with expectations. I love holidays, and in my mind, I get two (my birthday and Mother's Day—I know I'm not alone in this). My mind was trained on my big day and my simple requests, "Feed me at home and cook it." It started out not going the way I had hoped. I started feeling hurt and disappointed as the morning went on.

I had forgotten that my husband was under a lot of pressure regarding an extremely important meeting the following day. He was getting cushions out and setting up the patio so we could spend time outside for what turned out to be a lovely day.

When my son arrived to make breakfast, I knew I was going to be late for church at best. Fortunately, he made mimosas, which I wouldn't normally drink before church. But yes! I'll have two, thank you very much!

Had I asked one question, and considered my husband's context, I would have remembered how much pressure he was under. I would have better appreciated the efforts he made. He was loving me in his love language which is acts of service. Had I asked one question, I would've known what my son had to push through to get the groceries and arrive at my home to cook. He was loving me in one of his love languages — giving gifts. When I did see it, I spoke to them in my love language which is words of affirmation. I made a point to thank them and tell them I really had enjoyed all that they had done, making the patio beautiful and sitting outside all afternoon, and shopping for and preparing a delicious breakfast. My other son had work, so I heard from him later in the day. He sang a song with lyrics he had rewritten for me – it was beautiful. When I looked at that day through the lens of context, I saw that I was being loved despite the pressure, roadblocks, and schedules my family was under. They deserved double credit for pushing through to love me—even from their native tongues,

Being Fully Present

We've all experienced people looking at their electronic devices instead of us while carrying on a conversation (maybe we're guilty of this ourselves!). You know what a difference it makes when your friend silences their phone and puts it out of sight to focus on the present moment. Isn't it affirming when someone sets aside all the distractions of the day to focus entirely on you? It's especially important during conflict resolution to be attentive to the subject and the person.

To fully engage, be sure to share your thoughts and feelings. This is part of the process of being known and expanding intimacy with your partner, family member, or friend. You cannot have true intimacy with someone you don't fully know or withhold information from. And you can't be fully known (and accepted) if you don't share your mind and heart, fears, hopes, and expectations. But to do so, it requires that two people create a safe haven for their relationship.

Nurturing your common belief systems is one way to do that. These are the big umbrella values like faith and family that you both share. So if you both have a common faith paradigm, then you may have similar views, outcomes, or goals on forgiveness. Maybe you share the belief that forgiveness is infinite, "seventy times seven," thus, your attitude and efforts toward forgiveness and restoration will be continuous.

Another shared value may be morality. Within a monogamous framework, how does each person in the relationship define loyalty? Depending on a person's life experience, maybe it's not safe for the other person to have lunch with someone of the opposite sex. For others, flirting may not be okay. For some, it might be fine as long as you look and don't touch. Determine what you agree on regarding how relationships will be handled with the opposite sex. Loyalty includes confidences. What is appropriate to share about each other's past or present?

What are your common foundations? It is important to nurture your common ground in all relationships. It's important to establish definitions early to avoid conflict later.

Cultural Awareness

Every relationship entity or culture is defined by common language, history, and traditions. There are phrases that those who share in that culture understand, that outsiders may not. There are rituals that you perform every day that keep things together. When these rituals fall off, there's a break in the culture.

For example, you have a way you come and go when leaving for work or coming home. If a husband normally kisses his wife upon waking, or just before going to work and says, "I love you," and he fails to do this, the wife is going to notice. There's a break in the pattern that needs to be addressed. Routines help us to see that.

Culture contains many things: how you celebrate holidays, the foods you eat, the conversations you have, and how you spend time. Your culture usually comes from families of origin. In partnerships and marriages there will usually be a blend of both.

By conducting regular check-in meetings, people know they'll have an opportunity to air their concerns and wounds or see where they're breaking the culture pattern. It prevents small issues from becoming much bigger issues that can cause bigger conflicts. It also fosters understanding with the other person in the relationship.

Curiosity or Judgment?

In Terry Fadem's book *The Art of Asking*, he dives into how to ask the questions that get better answers. People generally ask questions for curiosity or ask questions for judgment.

A former client to whom I recommended this book gave me permission to share his thoughts. "When I first read this book, I didn't understand that there were better ways of asking than my way. I couldn't figure out how to ask questions in a way that didn't have some level of judgment attached. That book helped me see that I wasn't asking for curiosity. I asked in a way that told you what I thought. It certainly carried judgment because that's really where I was coming from. It takes some time to see and hear how we ask our questions so that we can reword them to get the information we really want."

I developed a therapeutic tool that I made into a game. I called it Ask One More Question and tried it out on my family. The rules of the game are that before you assume anything, you have to ask one more question. You can even solicit help from the other person.

If you're in the middle of a conflict, or there's tension, you may not know what question to ask. If you don't have a question, you can say, "I need a question," or ask, "Can you give me a question?" The other person can ask, "Do you need to ask a question?" or, "Would you like to ask one more question?" But you must ask at least one more before jumping to a conclusion. My family played it and I found it really did sensitize as to how quickly we make assumptions without getting any information.

One afternoon, I came home knowing that one of my sons was planning to go out. I was barely inside the door and immediately he says, "Bye Mom!"

"Wait! Time out! You know you can't go anywhere until your room has been clean. Make sure you go and clean your room." I hadn't asked him anything. I had no more information than an assumption that he had not cleaned his room (based on relevant history). I suspected he was using his charm and loving on mom to get out the door.

"I think you need to ask one more question," he

said. I backed up to start all the way over, realizing I hadn't even greeted him.

"Wow, I'm sorry."

"Hello, Mom."

"Hi, son. How are you doing? I know that you have plans today. We had an agreement that there were some things you needed to do before you went. Did you have a chance to clean your room today?"

"Yes, I did!" Because he was still standing there, I asked one more question. "Would you like me to see what you've done?"

"I sure would."

He was so proud to take me up and show me how he had organized his shelves with an elaborate system he devised. The previous scenario could have left him feeling that he can't please Mom. Instead, I affirmed his effort and accomplishment, and he was validated.

Flatten the Conflict Curve

When we have a conflict, it's often not truly about the topic at hand. We think we're fighting *about* money, sex, time, tasks, or offenses, but we're really fighting about what it represents to each party. We are usually fighting *for* something. We fight *for* appreciation when we feel taken for granted. We fight *for* validation when we feel dismissed, we fight *for* attention when we feel neglected, or we have an unmet expectation that was never expressed. True resolution can occur when we understand the needs beneath the discord. What also sustains conflict is having expectations that we don't share with others, and then expect people to meet them. Until we know how to quantify and share our expectations, we can't expect anyone to meet them. What is our expectation? Why is it our expectation?

We have the opportunity to use conflicts as building blocks for intimacy if we can:

- gain clarity about our needs and the reasons behind them
- uncover unexpressed expectations
- have a willingness to compromise
- be curious to gain context

I remember an example of a frustration I had with my husband. When I got home later than he did, the outside lights weren't on, and the house was dark. Both of which—to me—felt dismissive and hurtful. He would go to bed early and go to sleep.

In his family, everyone came and went freely to

do what they needed to do. They were all very independent and trustworthy. His reflex was: I'm done for the day and closing it down. He's the guy who turns out lights not being used to avoid wasting resources. That's not unreasonable.

I finally asked, "Why did you turn out the lights?" After all, the lights being on was important to me. But as stated earlier, you can't know another person's thoughts unless they tell you. Just as you cannot read the minds of others, you must ask yourself, are you expecting others to read your mind?

Back to the Ladder of Integrity, it wasn't until I untangled what lights on or off meant to me that I could express myself to my husband. What did lights off mean to me? My narrative was, "You don't care if I come home. You don't care about my safety." I put a lot of meaning and pain on that single action.

In my family, I was taught you leave the porchlight on until everyone is home safely. It means your return is anticipated and welcomed. It means that the home is not closed until everybody is home. It means we care about each other's safety, so we leave a light on at the door so you can see to get in. You leave a light on in the hall, so you can move freely without hazard.

"I didn't know it meant all that!" he replied. "Of course, I'll leave them on! No, I don't want you to fall on your way in."

Neither of us had thought about it from the other person's perspective until we had a conversation about it. Then we were able to understand what leaving the lights on meant to me and what turning them off meant to him. None of it had anything to do with love or care. So many relationships have narratives of hurt, neglect, dismissal, etc., over things that are actually a lack of context, unexamined and unexpressed expectation, and a lack of clarity around their own needs. Thus, we misinterpret.

Now he leaves on a night light and a hall light. Not only that, but he also leaves on my bedside lamp and the sheets are folded down. Because he can fall asleep under any circumstance, he may not even hear me come in. But even while he's asleep, he has welcomed me home and to bed. (And I turn lights off as I pass each one, so we don't waste resources.)

For Your Consideration

1. Which of the tools you've read about in this chapter can you use now to benefit your current relationships?
2. Assume you don't know. Ask one more question.
3. In your most recent conflict, what changes if you consider it in a different context?

13 Forgiveness

My husband and I went on an amazing vacation with friends to the beautiful Maslina Resort in Croatia, tucked in the middle of a pine forest on the island Hvar. Aside from being private and beautiful, what made this secluded destination attractive was the Mediterranean meals made with locally farmed ingredients. The artistic design of the resort and wellness center included beautiful natural materials like wood, terra cotta, and stone. Each room revealed a stunning and calming view of the Adriatic Sea.

On our last day, I went to the spa to investigate their local health customs. Up to then, I hadn't done sound therapy, which included bells, glass or stone bowls, and reflexology. As part of my massage, they offered a selection of aromatherapy scents to choose from. The attendant explained each one, along with their beneficial effects, as well as the popular aromas. When I chose my scent, she said the most interesting thing.

"The people who choose that are usually holding onto something, because to them it smells good. But to most people, it stinks. So if it doesn't stink to you. . ."

Initially, I thought, "Okay that's a little out there." As she massaged my feet, she gently asked questions.

"Are you harboring unforgiveness?"

My first thought was, "Sis, you don't know how much work I've done to get where I am right now. I'm an educated clinician, and intuitive and.... Hmmm. I mentally ticked through a list. My marriage was in a strong place, and I had a close circle of trusted friends. Although several years before there had been struggles with a number of relationships, I was on much more solid footing. I knew very well the importance of forgiving and boundaries and had found a measure of peace waiting for me on the other side, which I was currently enjoying. So I gave her my most truthful answer.

"I don't think so."

Maybe because my body was so relaxed, I let

my mind wander and began to consider her question. Whatever she said next started me weeping. As I thought more about it, I realized I had not forgiven myself for my part in previous conflicts, or for feeling stupid. Several other important areas of my life came to my attention. Suddenly, shocking imagery rushed into my mind; things with my parents I hadn't thought about in decades. It felt almost overwhelming. I needed to deeply ponder and untangle them.

On that last night of our vacation, nobody wanted anymore fancy dinners. They just wanted to go down and have pizza and wine on the wall, where they could enjoy another gorgeous view of the water. Preoccupied with my thoughts, I decided against going along.

The massage therapist had hit on something just beyond my grasp. I was so haunted by what had unfolded during the massage, I wanted to be alone to journal and think about it. I allowed myself to feel the emotions and named them: shame and regret. I brought my mind to my emotions. I felt stupid and a little frustrated because I didn't want to still be in the process of forgiving anything. I wanted to be done forgiving. But even this is part of elevated self-care.

Bring Your Mind to Emotions

Journaling not only gives you a safe place to vent, but it also makes your thoughts into things you can act upon. It activates another part of the brain that is solution oriented. The action of putting a pen to paper is calming. Keeping journals benefits you in other ways. They're a record of the tests you go through, and for some, it reveals how God shows up in challenging circumstances. Journals also reveal how you've grown through the toughest times of your life. Written words offer a way to view your experiences over time, evaluate your thought process, see patterns of behavior, and understand what's important to you.

As a counselor and coach, I've observed the difference in impact between when something happens to you by happenstance – such as an accident or diagnosis—and when something happens on purpose such as betrayal by a friend, spouse or relative. In the former, you absorb the shock, learn how to adjust, form a plan, and grieve its many parts.

A betrayal, for instance, is usually intentional and cruel. It has far-reaching ramifications. Navigating those consequences is not a small thing. And to navigate it well, we must consider forgiveness.

There are varying degrees of forgiveness. Forgiveness doesn't automatically mend the situation, restore trust, or resolve hurt feelings. Forgiving doesn't mean you're condoning hurtful behavior. You can forgive people to different ends. You may choose to forgive unto restoration, or you may choose to disallow access or erect a boundary.

Forgiveness and grieving go hand in hand. The forgiveness process is very similar to grief, in that it's different for everyone and isn't fully defined. It's a process of grieving and releasing and forgiving. You grieve all that is lost in any betrayal. You release yourself and those who hurt you. You forgive yourself for not seeing possibly obvious clues, feeling blindsided or victimized, then release those feelings. I've distilled forgiveness down to some key elements:

- Understand that forgiveness is for you.
- Forgiving doesn't excuse what happened to you.
- Self-forgiveness is part of that process.

All of this takes time.

Pursuing Freedom

No matter what the offense is, no matter the type or

how long it went on, you don't heal from anything you won't feel or look at. It means feeling uncomfortable emotions like anger, shock, disappointment, or deep hurt. Take the time to name each of your feelings regarding the offense.

When you've been harmed, it disturbs your equilibrium. Part of your need is to restore some sort of balance. You may even want retribution. Write down your thoughts and make them things. Write out all your feelings and name what you lost. You may feel locked down with hurt feelings, but you can gain freedom as you recognize you're not responsible for the other person's decisions. You don't own that. Initially, you may want the other person to feel that same level of hurt, or to at least acknowledge the level of pain they've caused. It's okay to admit that to yourself; that's a normal reaction but not a solution.

Forgiving someone who wounded you seems counterintuitive. It may feel like you're letting them get away with it. In cases of abuse, telling someone to forgive their abuser shortcuts some very important processes and may not even be reasonable, healthy, or achievable. The abused would feel a strong, uncomfortable sense that they were excusing that person. There's nothing excusable about abuse of any sort.

What came to me during that massage in Croatia was a truth about my family of origin. We looked great. My dad had achieved far beyond expectations; my mom was elegant and engaging. They were the shiny and successful ones in the family. My dad was a big man, over six feet tall, two hundred fifty pounds, very handsome, witty, and, by all accounts, a kind and motivational leader. My mom was shapely, stylish and petite. She was well-read, wise, generous, and hospitable.

However, our family was a mess. My parents had a rough marriage. You could cut the tension with a knife and their fights at times escalated to shouting and shoving. At times, we kids felt fear, insecurity, and anger. We hated it, so much so that each of us kids individually and collectively asked them to divorce.

But somehow, over the decades, my parent's marriage was eventually healed. This is where my hope for relationships is rooted. They enjoyed trips together and being silly together. My mom seemed happier than I had ever seen her. I knew there had been incredible healing. I don't know if they went to counseling or anything about their process. I wish I did. There was clearly a lot of work done and forgiveness must have been foundational.

Forgiveness doesn't set your offender free of responsibility. In your valley of decision, you can choose to forgive because it sets *you* free. Forgiveness is choosing to be free from carrying a hurt that will never be paid for. It likely won't be a one-and-done forgiveness, but *many decisions* to forgive. It's important to be patient with the process and remember that forgiving heals you. Forgiveness is soul-care.

Deciding to Forgive

Forgiveness is two-fold, repetitive, and cyclical. It's a decision or series of decisions, and a process. Every time the hurt rises in you, you can choose to enter the forgiveness process—it is repetitive and thus a cycle. At the beginning this is difficult—and may seem impossible. However, it gets better as you move along the path.

Wanting the offender to acknowledge the hurt they caused or to feel that level of hurt means you expect something from the offender. Here's a newsflash: True forgiveness needs nothing from the offender. Forgiveness is not getting their apology or whether they acknowledge the pain they caused.

No matter what they say, it won't undo the damage. The past can't be put right. It happened, it's done, and it can't be redone.

Forgiveness is acknowledging that you no longer look to the offender for your healing. Your part, as the injured party, is to stop going to them. Release the idea that they can fix it or make right what they did. You learn to accept and make peace with what happened.

The self-care of forgiveness is how we process our hurt. Even after forgiveness has done its work, it still isn't about those who hurt you. It's about deciding to take care of yourself and process your emotional hurt and mental anguish in a healthy way.

In forgiveness unto restoration, the offender participates in rebuilding the relationship. If both people choose to move forward together toward healing a relationship, both people must contribute. It's not enough for the offender to admit it and own their actions, but they must learn to appreciate the magnitude of the impact. Their contribution requires participating in laying the groundwork for healing or providing the atmosphere for healing. Participating in restoration means acknowledging and facing the pain of the hurt person, not hiding from the feelings those actions caused. While the offender can't heal the wounds they caused, they can be open and available to discuss the issue ad nauseum, and not get in the way, until the hurt person has fully processed them.

Many times, I hear the offender say, "But we've covered that!" That may be true, but for some individuals, talking about a problem is like looking at a document on the computer screen. After the discussion, it's like the window is closed. For other individuals, the window is still open. And there might be a lot of windows still open. That individual might be going back and forth between those open windows, gathering, and processing information and seeking meaning. A topic may have been discussed and yet remain unresolved. Not until that window is closed can you move on to another subject.

All parties should seek to be on the same page as to what resolution or reconciliation looks like. One may feel unresolved and the other may feel it's been over-processed. The one who feels that the situation has been more than duly processed must provide empathetic space in their heart and mind to allow the unresolved person to get closer to resolution. It probably won't look like, "We both agree!" That rarely happens. But it's necessary to respect the other person and accept that they have a different process.

And finally, but of equal importance, what if you are the person who has offended and needs to be forgiven? These principles still apply. Consider how you will acknowledge your actions and face the pain you caused. Recognize that you cannot fix what you broke. You can, however, participate and be willing to contribute to a healing atmosphere and, if necessary, talk it through until it's through; whether you participate unto reconciliation or to a boundary, whether or not you're not allowed back into their life.

Once you've asked for forgiveness and offered your patient participation in their healing process — you're free. If they choose to deny you access, or choose not to forgive you, you're released. You don't have to live under condemnation for your worst decisions the rest of your life.

No one can dictate your process — it may be longer; it may be shorter. However, it is wise to cultivate an understanding and a tolerance for the differences. Those with a longer process must also understand and validate that others may not need all that time.

Treasure in the Tempest

Even if you bear the painful consequences of someone else's choices, a significant part of the healing and forgiveness process is taking the courageous step to look at some of your own stuff.

I believe that anything you give to God, He'll use. So look for the gift in the circumstance. Sometimes it's the gift of seeing things in yourself that you might never have seen otherwise. We might even need to ask for forgiveness and then forgive ourselves.

When people look at their stuff, their relationships can become even better. It's unbelievable how much better! Of course, we wish certain conflicts and offenses never happened, but if you go through the process, you can expose unseen strengths that allow the relationship to flourish.

I've seen numerous marriages healed over time. Remembering my parent's marriage, I have proof that really difficult dynamics can heal. I choose to believe that anything is possible, a belief I carry into my work as a clinician. It's one reason I love working with couples. It's very hard to change the way you think, and to be accountable, but I have seen it happen. If you really want to, it can be done.

Choosing the Outcome

It bears repeating that an important question regarding forgiveness is whether to let the offender back into your life. Forgive and forget is an unrealistic, generally unachievable, and even dangerous standard. God may forget, but we do not forget. Offenses become part of our lived experience. Whether you choose to bring those people who hurt you back into your life or not—it's still freedom.

After I posted a similar message on social media, a woman messaged me. She'd had a painful experience with a family member. But because they were family, she thought she had to maintain the relationship. My post surprised her and left her asking, "You mean I don't have to?"

"Not if there's been no change." I asked her several important questions. "Where are you in this process? Are you still harboring resentment? Do you still feel the pain? Is it still tender? Tell me about your forgiveness."

She said it was fine but felt obligated to the larger family to avoid making this a big deal. But it was a big deal. It seemed like people wanted to overlook it and maintain the status quo. I told her she didn't owe them her peace and safety.

For Your Consideration

1. Your next courageous step could be not doing this alone, but with a therapist. What are the feelings that you don't want to feel, or that make you uncomfortable? Write them down and make them things.

2. How will your life look once you've forgiven the person who hurt you? Or who you hurt? Write out how you see it unfolding.

3. What have you learned about yourself through examining this process!

SPIRITUAL

14 Inspiration

As I look out the window this morning, I notice the beauty of creation. The leaves are changing on the trees in the woods, and they almost look like stained glass the way the sun shines through them. Just beyond, light twinkles like stars on the lake. My sanctuary is just below the window I'm gazing from, in the center of that amazing view. That space, where I've written so many gratitudes, is the place where I can quiet my mind and hear from God and be inspired. That's where my heart longs to be. Inspiration recharges me.

I'm a person who moves a lot and finds myself in the midst of near-constant activity around me. While watching my beloved granddaughter, I don't have the time to be still in my mind. Paired with the goings on of late, I feel depleted. When I find myself in such a condition, I allow myself periods of not moving. Stillness of body can be brought on by many things: exhaustion, pain or needing a pause. However, stillness of body is not the same as being still in the mind. Stillness of mind requires intentionality.

When still, I can be inspired in ways that are unobtainable when I'm on-the-go. For me, inspiration is like breath, and it's essential in the way breathing is essential.

We've probably all used the phrase, "So and so is inspiring." Various people might have said to you, "Your message made me feel so inspired!" And while I've been touched by those kind words myself, it didn't occur to me to ask, "What do you mean? Inspired how? Did it just feel good in the moment? Did it motivate you to do something different or to think differently? Did it provoke you to ponder something more deeply?"

Inspiration can come from almost anywhere. Some people who currently inspire me are in the similar public spaces that I'm called to occupy. They're mature women in their fifties, sharing why they do what they're doing. One shares a message that women over fifty can have great experiences, and be fun and fashionable, all while displaying their crown of gray hair. Their stories capture my attention.

Each is motivational, encouraging and sharing an important life-stage message, which resonates with me. Each of them packages their similar messages differently. They speak to a place where I've felt fear or insecurity. One train of thought that seems to get in my way is a limiting belief about age. These inspirational women speak to barrier breaking, being courageous, and the advantages of lived experience. They encourage me by providing more than one reason to keep moving forward. They motivate me with their creativity and grace.

At times, their reasons resonate with mine. My motivation, my justification, my default, is that I really love people and want them to experience freedom, richness in their relationships, enjoyment in life, peace from God, and gratitude. My reasons stem from a desire to live out God's investment in me. Each of my motivators had some obstacle to overcome in their own lives. Because they did, others find hope in their messages.

Jesus said we should approach the kingdom of Heaven like a child. There's something powerful in that childlike wonder. While spending time with my granddaughter, I notice how present she is. She eats when she's hungry, and cries when she's hurt or needs help. She doesn't have any limitations, and has no fear of judgment—she simply makes her needs known. She sleeps when she's tired and wakes up singing when she's refreshed. What would life be like to wake up singing? How can I be that present in daily life?

Even when we walked several times around the same tree, every moment she saw something new. Every leaf on the ground was something amazing and wonderous to explore. She inspired me to look at being in the moment. She's not afraid of running out of time. She just is. What happens to us that we lose our childlike wonder? Through inspiration, we can get some of that back.

Capturing Inspiration

It's too easy to get distracted from good sources of information when constantly running. Recently, I shot a new podcast episode with a guest from my first season, who shares her aggregate news program on various social media platforms. I wanted to talk about how much she's evolved since we last met two years ago. She had a clarity and lightness in her countenance that was neat to observe. I asked about her process to get to this better place, where she's able to do even more than before.

She'd spent the first year trying many things to

get people to pay attention to her message. Afterward, she chose to get still and took a month off. In social media-land, that's a long time. During this sabbatical, she realized that she'd been listening to some limiting messages. Believing them instead of trusting herself, she'd lain some things down that she really liked.

The next year, she took two months off. In the social media world, where folks are used to hearing from you every day, maybe several times a day, that's truly an eternity — she didn't care. Her priority was getting answers and clarity. Her comeback plan contained the caveat that if her following didn't return, that would be an answer and the impetus to do something else. However, though not the way she expected, her following did return. The respite freed her to do more. Her new, sharper insight allowed her to expand that which fed her soul. The breakthrough she gained by being still more than made up for anything that had been lost in her absence.

This Present Stillness

The importance of getting still cannot be overstated. Many inventors, creatives and problem solvers have paused, or taken naps and dreamed their solutions while sleeping. Being still provides you with time to collect your thoughts and release pressure, which engages a different part of the mind—the part that delivers answers and inspiration. Take the time to hear from yourself and acknowledge your thoughts. Validate those thoughts by making them things—writing them down and taking small action steps. You can inspire yourself.

Inspiration in its purest form leaves its imprint upon you—a fresh perspective that challenges you to grow. If you embrace it, you'll never be the same. You can be uplifted and see something in a new way or be stirred toward some action or visible change. You may be flooded with new innovations and emboldened to try something you once feared.

Inspiration can allow you to see yourself in a different light and enable you to appreciate your quirks and distinctions. Self-awareness and authenticity will grow hand in hand, producing a fullness in your soul. You'll want to be present. You'll want to know yourself as you were created to be. It means being aware and accepting of self on an emotional, physical, and thought level. You can't take care of a self you don't know. I love the saying, "God can't heal/use/grow the person you pretend to be."

It's been stated that many people think they're self-aware when really, they're self-conscious. Self-consciousness is a preoccupation with self, whereas self-awareness is the ability to observe yourself with honesty and acceptance of the whole. What you learn about yourself informs how you move forward in every aspect of your daily life.

For example, if I don't keep certain habits in place, like what I eat and what I wear, they affect my mood. They affect my physical and emotional health and how I show up in other areas with my family or friends. When I make plans without considering the health consequences, I suffer. I've learned to make every effort to consistently be authentic especially with myself.

I'm not advocating self-awareness for the purpose of pre-occupation. I'm encouraging you to understand yourself because the Creator of All purposed you to be here. How well do you know that person?

You came into this world naked and alone. You were born into a family system, given a name, and over time collected people and roles. But you aren't leaving this life as a role. You're leaving as the naked you, the way you came in, the individual God created. How are you nurturing, caring for, and inspiring that person's life? Part of your mission is to properly maintain and motivate that individual so that you can live out your purposes. What are your sources for that?

Many people believe (as I do) that the Bible is the inspired word of God. I've experienced God in ways I can't prove with scripture, but they're not out of alignment. I know God still does miracles because I've had miraculous experiences. I have many examples where God showed me that He purposed me to be here.

Because I tend to minimize what I do, I'm not always aware of how God uses me to impact or inspire others. Yet, I believe I've been collecting inspiration all my life in order to do so. Through my podcasts and this book, I hope to inspire people, but I have trepidation about asking others if I've inspired them. Occasionally, someone will send me a message, "Your comments are always a place of inspiration." Instead of asking them, "How do you mean?" I say thank you. If others inspire me by being authentic, then I can do the same by living authentically and sharing my story. And so can you.

Where Inspiration Lives

The root word of inspiration is the French word *spirare* meaning to breathe. Breath does good things for us: it revives, cleanses, recenters and calms us. I like that as a metaphor. When you find yourself in unfamiliar situations, take a breath. Breathing can take you from tense moments of panic to moments of problem-solving peace.

Much of what inspires me has come from stillness and observation. However, watching how people move, speak and handle situations can provide alternatives for how we want to be (or not be). It was in the still moments that I began noticing how much my mother influenced me. She was truly not a respecter of persons and talked to all regardless of race or social distinction. She could talk to somebody on the street with just as much warmth and interest as the person on a committee, or a person of high status. My mother valued people and many of them loved her. Her kind regard of people was something I aspired to emulate in my own life.

While the Bible has long been a go-to source of inspiration for me, countless books also touch on nearly any subject that interests you. Numerous online sites are devoted to inspirational quotes that can become mantras or words to live by. The written word is very powerful. Making declarations, repeating verses, and even writing words down will help you integrate them into your thought life.

Observing nature and the amazing creation we

live in is another vast source of inspiration and healing for millions, including myself. How often you make it a part of your routine is up to you, but if you love it, make room for it. Part of your self-care might already include spending time in the great outdoors. You may be inspired by architecture, cityscapes, and museums. Inspiration is in the air. It's everywhere. Walk out your front door, go somewhere new, or sit by a body of water. Find your quiet self. Be present in the moment. Just breathe.

For Your Consideration

1. We talked about some podcasters that have inspired me. What are your sources for inspiration?

2. In what way did it inspire you? What was changed as a response?

3. In what way(s) have you inspired another person?

15 Gratitude

"There will come a point in time when you can find things to be grateful for. It will be a cue to you that you are on the path to healing." I'd said this to a young woman some time ago. When going through a very difficult time in her marriage, she recited my own sage advice back to me; words she used as a barometer of her own healing. The timing was interesting too. I had just begun writing this chapter on gratitude when she confessed to keeping a gratitude journal. She wanted to share with me some things she was grateful for.

"I'm still grateful for my marriage because the pain is making me into a woman I respect; and it's bringing me closer to God. Also, I'm happy I got to be a mom. Because according to my body, I shouldn't have been able to get pregnant. My husband and child have been huge blessings. Through God, they have made me grow up."

The concept of gratitude is profound but simple. It raises personal awareness and transcends religion. It's more of an attitude and less of a spiritual belief. In recent years, there's been a growing trend to keep gratitude journals. Like many trends, their impact can be minimized as just a fad. I strongly believe in making your thoughts things. As a clinician I often recommended that people do directed journaling, but I rarely made gratitude the focus.

My first example of seeing gratitudes written out was after my mother passed. I read what she'd journaled after I had received my first cancer diagnosis at seventeen. I gained insight by seeing how she worked through that crisis, how she processed the report, and what she did and didn't say, from counting her blessings to the Bible verses she chose to copy.

My own gratitude journal was inspired by my mother's example. I was sensitized to the concept back in grad school, many years later. But it wasn't until the wheels fell off my own life that I initiated my own daily practice.

Retuning Focus

In my pursuit to gain some footing and understanding, I, too, began journaling. My goals were uncomplicated: write out three to five things a day for which I was grateful. This helped me break out of a fear and despair mindset by searching for what is true, beautiful, lovely, and those things of good report. The first few days of this new commitment were easy. When it wasn't so simple, I reminded myself this is a discipline.

That first year, starting in early spring, our firepit down by the water became my sanctuary. Somehow, even though it rained every morning, it was always warm enough and dry enough for me to sit outside. I'd grab my journal, my blue tooth speaker and my coffee and sit down there. In that place I was far enough away that I could cry and speak my mind out loud to God, who was my source of all things. There I felt hidden in the presence of God. This practice continued into late fall.

Some days, finding the simplest thing to be grateful for was hard. Also, I wanted to be creative and have fresh gratitudes to write about, not the same few things every day. To maintain the discipline, I freed myself from that limitation. I'd write about whatever I could find to be grateful for that was not connected to my current situation. Gratitude is recognizing that I am not entitled to the good that comes to me. I realized that anything good that I have is sent intentionally from a source of good. For me, that is God.

I found myself watching for things to be grateful for. Not all were big shiny moments; often they were simple. Grateful the rain stopped. Grateful for a cup of coffee. Grateful for breath. Once, I was even grateful for the experience of pain, caused by a biting mosquito, because it let me know, "I'm alive and can feel."

Gratitude journaling was the beginning of many things for me in the self-care, soul-care space. It helped me begin owning my feelings and thoughts in ways I hadn't before. It raised my awareness of what I was feeling in my body to a higher level. There were times I thought, "I can't breathe!" I had an awareness of the source of my every breath. This brought to mind the song "Breathe" a song by Marie Barnett. It was good to take stock of all the good I currently enjoyed, and that which showed up every day.

Thankfulness vs. Gratitude

Although thankfulness is similar to gratitude, gratitude holds an element of extra appreciation, and much more weight. A person who faces their mortality or survives a life-threatening diagnosis, experience, or loss, develops a deeper appreciation for life. I see gratitude as a heart posture that is planted from a higher power and is cultivated from within. It exists without regard to circumstance, even though it often grows in response to pain. Thankfulness is a good thing. However, I see it as a thought-level response to something external and typically painless. It carries an element of courtesy in response to a kind or generous act. I'm thankful for my birthday gift, but I'm grateful for the relationship with the friend who gave it to me.

All life is precious, but the survivor can have a deeper level of appreciation for it because they've had to ponder its loss in real time. Gratitude appreciates not only what is—but what was nearly lost. While fighting for my life more than once, there were no guarantees that I would survive. I didn't expect to be here now at sixty. No matter what happens, whether difficulties with family or friends, heartache, pain, or emotional state—I'm still grateful to wake up. I'm aware that I'm living in bonus.

I choose to experience all that I could have missed.

We've all lost people who were important to us; they were here one day and gone the next. We loved them and cared about them. While those cherished people cannot be replaced, it provides the perspective that we must be mindful of not taking for granted the people who love us and ones we love. Gratitude is rooted in being aware of our context and the people within it. Rather than being caught up in the constant pursuit of what we don't yet have, gratitude focuses on all that we do have.

Gratitude is a mindset and a discipline. Recording in some way what you're grateful for helps you maintain a hopeful attitude through the tough times. By affirming the many things for which you are grateful, you're boosting your spiritual self-care.

Significant Sources

Encouragement and inspiration can be found in several sources. Early on, I wrote down pages of scriptures—just like my mom—and let it soak into my mind, heart, and soul by reading and writing them, making them my thoughts. I had my personal go-to verses that provoked real soul searching.

> In his grace, God has given us different gifts for doing certain things well. So if God has given you the ability to prophesy, speak out with as much faith as God has given you. If your gift is serving others, serve them well. If you are a teacher, teach well. If your gift is to encourage others, be encouraging. If it is giving, give generously. If God has given you leadership ability, take the responsibility seriously. And if you have a gift for showing kindness to others, do it gladly.
>
> Don't just pretend to love others. Really love them. Hate what is wrong. Hold tightly to what is good. Love each other with genuine affection, and take delight in honoring each other. Never be lazy, but work hard and serve the Lord enthusiastically. Rejoice in our confident hope. Be patient in trouble, and keep on praying. When God's people are in need, be ready to help them. Always be eager to practice hospitality. Romans 12: 6-13

After writing them, I meditated on specific phrases: *Don't pretend to love others. Really love them.* Do I love, God? Or am I pretending to love? What is true? Was I hating what is wrong and holding tightly to what is good?

During difficult seasons, you don't want to ignore or suppress your pain. Give honor to the hurt; feel it and name it. But take care not to let it rule you. In God's grace, we're able to do many things that otherwise seem impossible.

The discipline of gratitude journaling precipitated the greatest freedom and growth season in my self-awareness. It helped clear my mind and order my thoughts. It revealed to me things that I would never have had the courage to try before, like the podcasts or writing this book. They might never have existed if the bottom hadn't fallen out of my life.

There were self-revelations that I would have missed because I was not incentivized to look at what was underneath. As I sifted through my areas of co-dependence, I discovered how it's wrapped up in layers of high-functioning good stuff that makes people around me feel good. I now see what was wounded, or broken, or dysfunctional at my core. God knew there was only one way that I was ever going to see it. It needed to be shaken out of me. I needed an earthquake.

Journaling strengthened my belief that God will use whatever you give Him — if you give it to

Him. Writing out daily gratitudes is big part of giving those concerns over to Him.

Acknowledging the Good

Gratitude is how I move forward when things are hard or inconvenient. It also prevents me from taking things for granted when all is well. The discipline of gratitude journaling was useful in and of itself to control my thoughts; it caused me to intentionally search for and find those things outside of my situation — negative or otherwise. Gratitude helped me discover and own my thoughts and experiences, my presence and place in the world.

The practice of writing gratitudes and being still connected me with God. It reminded me of my love for Him, my history with Him and my worth in Him. God is always my go-to.

When I got my second cancer diagnosis, I remember screaming to God in my living room at three or four in the morning. "What are we doing? I thought we did this already!" When I was in pain the other night, I screamed at God. But that's who I always turn to.

I rehearse my history with God because in Deuteronomy 6:7-9 he says, "Repeat them again and again to your children. Talk about them when you are at home and when you are on the road, when you are going to bed and when you are getting up. Tie them to your hands and wear them on your forehead as reminders. Write them on the doorposts of your house and on your gates."

I remember those instances that were so important to me because they're my treasures; they reveal the intimate care God provides not only to me, but to all individuals who call upon Him.

Years later, still writing out gratitudes, I'm in a better place now, mentally, physically, and spiritually. When I fall off, I notice a shift in my mood. When things get busy, or the unexpected comes up, I do fall off. When I realize it, I make every effort to get back to it. There are still days I struggle to find three things to be grateful for. Then there are days where I fill a whole page. Sometimes they're deeply meaningful as in having a successful but difficult conversation with a family member. Other times, they're very basic: grateful for waking up, for sunshine, and for waking up with a purpose.

Because I've hung onto my journals, I periodically go back and read them. It's encouraging to see growth and change over time. It helps me track what I thought was important and how that has shifted or taken on new depth. The understanding I've gained is worth the time and effort. It also proved to me that this is not a trend, but a barely tapped resource for living an examined life.

For Your Consideration

1. As you look at your day or even past week, what three to five things can you pull out to be grateful for?

2. How do you define your sources of power, goodness, and benevolence?

3. What circumstance occurring right now could benefit from the discipline of gratitude journaling? What, if anything, is preventing you from doing this today? What step can you take now, to make this part of your daily self-care?

16 Receiving Input

The self-improvement industry is alive and well because many of us know we need or desire to enhance certain troublesome aspects of our lives. Despite the courageous step forward to face our demons, receiving input on how to better ourselves isn't always easy to hear. In fact, sometimes, it's downright painful.

The concepts of input or contributing information, feedback and corrective action or critique are important in developing to your full potential. Reading this book and learning new processes is input. Feedback helps you track the best use of the new processes.

Corporate self-improvement resources are

dedicated to training employees how to receive input. Maybe you've heard of the structured 360 programs that many businesses implement. Taking weeks to complete, those above you, below you, around you, and beside you are interviewed. They contribute information regarding how they perceive you handle certain things. It also requires your self-assessment: how do you see yourself and your interactions within various situations? The cumulative results are then discussed to assist you in reconciling and processing the information. It may require making adjustments in behaviors or thinking, but the goal is to help you be an optimized version of yourself. Receiving input and feedback is, in many ways, a skill.

Evaluating Resources

From the time we're very small, we like hearing people tell us how wonderful we are. I take pictures of my granddaughter every time she visits. When she and I are together, she wants to look at my phone to see the pictures and videos of herself. It's natural for you to want to know about yourself. The inherent risk in getting input is that many people have received input which has been unkind, hurtful, and damaging. Things we've absorbed as truth is where a lot of your wounds come from. As a result, you may go to great lengths to avoid hearing negative things about sensitive areas, whether it is about you directly, your relationships, your job, your diet, how you spend your money or how you parent your children.

Let's refer again to the Johari Window model on page 25. You'll remember there's a quadrant where you know who you are privately and publicly. That knowledge is important. It helps you know how to sort new information that comes to you. Will you put that in your public persona, or keep it private? Knowing more about yourself allows you to choose how to use that information.

Keep in mind that we all have blind areas where others see us more clearly than we could ever see ourselves. Without a mirror, you can't see your back. Input is like holding up a mirror, so you can see what your back looks like.

The difference is that some of our input sources aren't reliable or objective. Instead of holding up a mirror, they may show us a distorted image of us; or if they have a hidden agenda, they might hold up an image of themselves and say it's you. Sometimes it's well-meaning parents who don't have an agenda but may magnify a particular trait or talent and say, "This is who you are." If you don't have a way to receive or filter input, you might ignore the input box which will cause your growth to be stunted.

Even when it's good information from loved ones and trusted sources, it can still be hard to hear. What may drive you toward accepting negative-sounding truths, is when the circumstance you're in is more painful than facing the truth.

A perfect example is couples who come to marriage counseling to save their relationship — usually not when things are going well. One or both will have to hear hard truths about their shortcomings and work out practical solutions. By being more informed about themselves, they can make self-aware choices.

During the process of growth, maturation, and healing, most of us develop wisdom in discerning what we allow to stick and discard that which isn't useful. We learn who our safe and reliable sources are and develop relationships with those people.

Spiritual Sources

The fourth quadrant of the Johari Window model is the unknown unknown. The things about you that nobody knows and that you don't know about yourself. How do you access information that you don't know? I'm informed by my faith paradigm. This is where God speaks and reveals things to me. He may disclose information by using input from others. The woman who inspired me to try podcasting is a perfect example of that.

God may speak through dreams or arrange divine appointments or unlikely circumstances. This is how I came to be part of the amazing circle of women that is currently so supportive. And He can use a spiritually discerning spouse within the sacred bonds of marriage. Their input can still be hard to hear whether it's inspired or not. When it's a difficult message, it's worth remembering that you're on the same team, and this information is not given to cause harm. It's meant to hold up a mirror and meant for your good. If you're honest with yourself, you can admit that unless they're singing your praises, you may not really want to hear what the other person has to say. But it won't make the input any less true — or valuable.

I recall a conversation with loved one about how there was a season when they hated going to church because all they heard was how bad a person they were. They felt condemned every sermon for not better nurturing faith or spending enough time in the Bible or in prayer. With that as the filter, they left defeated every week. As they became healthier, their perspective broadened, and the church experience changed. Instead of seeing evidence of inadequacy, they received encouragement or instruction. Your current emotional state or narrative filters effect the way you interpret input and feedback, whether you receive it as instructive or critical.

Opposing Input

I'm part of a larger circle of people whose input I trust. I also trust myself. I've reached a point where I'm not afraid to hear things that I may not be ready to receive. I can read books written from a lens that is not my own. I'm not afraid to listen to opposing information because I don't want to become a one-dimensional person. Without input, I realize I could very easily become cynical. Do I think being cynical protects me? Or am I putting up a mask?

Because we wear a lot of masks in our lives, our society, and our world, Paul Lawrence Dunbar's words in his poem "We Wear the Mask" still resonate with me. It was the pervasive understanding in black culture that we could not be ourselves and stay alive. Dunbar's reference to the mask—a smile—was as a tool necessary for survival. In similar fashion, we have places that we wear masks as protection, but they actually hide us from ourselves. What we really want is to be present and fully known.

Receptivity

Your state of mind has a lot to do with how you receive input and the sources you can receive from. If the voice in your head is of a critical mother, and that's all you know, you may not be able to heed the advice from an older woman. It's okay if you're not ready to go there. That's not safe for you yet. Even if the quantity and quality of her feedback is not that of your mom's. There may be other sources, a clinical counselor or even a book that can fill in. Your receptivity to feedback can change over time. Start with the safe sources. Absorb what you can and move forward from there.

For instance, let's say you're given a diagnosis from a medical professional that you have a debilitating illness. The first time you hear this news, it may feel like a life sentence. You may wonder how you'll navigate such a thing and be overwhelmed by the changes and adjustments that must be made to mitigate the effects.

Six months later, you meet with another medical specialist. This doctor has a warm smile and a winning personality, and his presentation of the same information is different. He points out how well you're doing, despite your condition. He may check other factors that play important supporting roles in your health, like maintaining your strength, observing good eating habits, and paying proper attention to your limitations. And he delivers the same news as the previous doctor and notes no changes in your condition. You perceive that this conversation is more hopeful. Same report but less painful. What changed?

It could be partly attributed to starting with positive statements. Another factor is that you've been managing the diagnosis for months, so you weren't afraid to hear what he had to say.

If the information isn't different, then the recipient must be. Over the course of time, your perspective has shifted. You may have a clearer idea of what this condition entails and are more receptive to a wider range of traditional and alternative methods of dealing with your health circumstance. With a mindset shift, the alternatives that were always present can now be explored.

Consider this personal example of a shift in receptivity. My husband wanted us to create a budget. At that time, my understanding of budget meant you're going to tell me what I can't do. My experience was with people who said they were on a budget and saying, "I can't do this or that because I'm on a budget." So, I wouldn't agree to it.

He mentioned giving me an allowance. The concept of him giving me an allowance sounded so restrictive! I didn't see any options in that. I projected my fear of being controlled onto him and was not going for it.

"Fine, you do the budget and give me an allowance," he countered.

He just wanted to know where the money went. Because he was willing to do that, it helped me see that a budget wasn't to control, but a way to tell your money where to go. It actually provided freedom. Once I agreed to do the budget, with allowances for both of us, it was as if our finances opened up. Suddenly we knew what our options were, and we could make the best-informed decisions. We planned for necessities and things that were important to each of us. The concept of being on a budget never changed but my paradigm shifted from seeing it as limiting to the freedom to manage cash flow. Once the mindset shifts, the options increase.

Internal Input

Naturally, input comes from outside sources, but it includes information you collect from examining your own experience. Moving through grief, difficult conversations, and relationships, even embracing moments of joy, is input and how you process it—regardless of the source—nurtures your soul.

Receiving input is the opposite of avoidance. You want to receive good and avoid that which hurts. While racking up input that's hurtful, you may have found yourself distancing from painful things. When you avoid hard conversations, you're in essence saying you don't want to receive. When you avoid things that hurt, they build up. To get healing and insight, you must go back and deal with it later. Because most of us want to be present in ourselves, and truly know ourselves, I've found several helpful tools. Keep in mind that none of these reveal your identity; they're simply a source of input. They may be useful in helping you dig out some patterns or gain insight about yourself.

The CliftonStrengths assessment helps to discover or confirm strengths and provide strategies that enable development of full potential.[3] This sort

---

[3] https://www.gallup.com/cliftonstrengths/en/254033/strengthsfinder.aspx

of information adds to self-awareness, validates giftings, and encourages you to try some things unfamiliar to you.

The DISC assessment is a personality tool that reveals Dominance, Influence, Steadiness and Compliance traits.[4] It may not be as much discovery as illumination, depending on where you are in life. My husband and I went to a DISC date night and were seated with only two other couples who had in common our dominant personality type. Eric and I were both influencers. "I" was our first letter. He was "ID" and mine was "IS." When we operate out of our strengths, we're powerful. People want to hear from us. We're influential in our own spaces and influential together. When we're healthy, we work to influence each other. This provided useful insight, confirmation, and affirmation.

Originally, I didn't want to do the controversial Enneagram.[5] Since a client asked me to, I read a book and went a little deeper. The purpose of this ancient personality profile is to uncover motivations, which are captured in a numbered personality type. If applied correctly, you look at motivations, not behaviors. It may be helpful to explore some of these surveys to gain more understanding

---

[4] https://www.discprofile.com/what-is-disc
[5] https://www.enneagraminstitute.com/type-descriptions/

of your motives.

These are just a few of the available tools from which you can receive input. I've found these helpful. The less threatened you feel about the underdeveloped or negative parts of your personality or history, the more able you are to receive input as encouragement rather than attack, and assessment rather than disapproval.

For Your Consideration

1. What area of your life, history, or personality is hardest for you to hear correction? Is this a recurring issue?

2. What or who is your most trustworthy source of input? What or who is the least?

3. If you could choose how to hear input that was hard to hear, knowing that it was meant to be helpful, what would you choose?

17 Moving Through

Society in general can be very impatient with the pain of others. Pushing folks to "get over it" or to move on is not usually in the best interest of the hurt party. This is especially true when it comes to processing big life events. When I hear people say it's time to move on, I usually feel a check in myself. To my clinical mind, "moving on" for the sole purpose of putting big events in the past suggests skipping over some necessary steps. I want to emphasize that *moving through* is an imperative part of a true healing process and significant to soul-care.

There are several benefits of moving through. For one, you can reclaim your power in areas where you felt powerless. Second, you can reclaim places where events occurred, which afford you the opportunity to create a new story.

An example of this is a client I had many years ago. We met because she was going through a horrible betrayal and devastating breakup. Her history was such that it had been a tremendous leap of faith to be in such an intimate and vulnerable space.

As a couple, they did many things together. They often walked certain routes, one of which was going to her favorite park near her home to sit together on a bench. For a while, my client couldn't bring herself to go there. In fact, because she couldn't bear driving by it, she went the long way home to avoid the street the park was on. After some time in therapy, I eventually shared my perspective.

"That street has done nothing to you, nor has the park, nor has the bench. You're treating them as though they injured you. How about thinking of how to reclaim those spaces? You liked that route! You liked that park. You loved that bench. You went there before you had a relationship with this person. Let's reclaim those spaces and create a new narrative."

My suggestion didn't dismiss that these favored places now felt soiled. However, the relationship was a brief moment of time in her history with this space. She needed to recognize her power to change that. We did cognitive behavioral therapy. She took careful notes to acknowledge and document what she felt.

The betrayal had triggered massive insecurities, lies and automatic negative thoughts about herself that she felt were true. She'd felt inadequate and never good enough for this person. Without giving credence to them she instead asked, "What might be a more reasonable, balanced thought? What's an alternative *positive* thought?" As she tracked her feelings, a pattern emerged. By continuing to ask questions, she created a different story. Little by little she reclaimed her spaces.

Eventually, she ran through that park again and stretched her legs at that bench. Had she not examined her feelings, her negative thoughts could have furthered a distorted narrative about herself. It could have become a permanent part of her story. By examining it, she took the useful and discarded the rest.

Taking the time to process provided her with powerful navigation tools for whatever else she may face. This is moving through, moving onward. It's healthy, restorative, and great self-care. For my client, that sad event was not the end. She went on, married, started a family, finished college, and moved forward with her life, healthy and purposed.

Managing the Cost

Those who say, "Just move on," aren't weighing the cost. Those things which you choose to ignore that go unprocessed never go away. At best, they go underground; but continue to affect other areas of your life until you deal with them. However, once you move through, you choose how much weight they carry.

Within your upbringing, certain things are part of your personality construct, and part of your perspective and development. They're not going to change. Even though your personality is solidified by age six or seven, you will mature in your expression and learn to respond appropriately as you grow in self-awareness.

I've mentioned before that I come from a family of wordsmiths. I can use my words to inflict pain or bring healing. Part of my personality is that I tend to be more reactive. When a certain part of my personality is triggered, I default to an established defense mechanism.

While that won't change, I've worked to release

that part. With self-awareness I can manage my reactions. Self-awareness gives me the time I need to make a conscious choice. (I don't always make that choice.) Through intention and grieving and working through all the things we've talked about thus far, I've created a space that I can stand in and speak from. I can ask myself, "Is this coming from a reactive need in me? Or am I providing help, or security for someone else?"

These days, most people experience me as gracious and gentle. I'm able to use my wordsmithing for good. I've been asked, "How did you know to say it that way?" The answer is training, practice, and a desire to watch my words. If a conversation gets difficult, I'm not afraid to say, "Can I get back to you on that?" Or I'll ask for a time-out to remove myself from the situation before I blow someone up. I've learned to practice the pause. I've learned to move through that reactive space, so it doesn't catch me up. I avoid creating another wound or another problem to deal with later on.

The benefit of self-awareness and continuing to grow and moving through is that with self-knowledge, they're not as frequent as before. When something doesn't go well, I use the tools to do a "postmortem." I look over the events realistically and ask myself what went wrong?

After you examine your thoughts at a time and a place, acknowledge and name what you feel, give weight to feelings, and fully validate the emotion that comes up in that moment, you can move on. Then you can leave in the past those things that you've taken the time and courage to move through.

Thoughts as Things

One of my favorite and most beneficial worksheets that I give to clients is the automatic thought record, which helps them make your thoughts into things. You can deal with whatever you can define. Let's say today you wake up and notice you're feeling down. What words describe your feelings? *I'm sad, tired, depressed, anxious.*

Maybe you woke up, had your morning coffee and now you're stuck. You feel like crying and aren't sure what's going on inside. What are your circumstances? Find words to name the emotions you're having. Give weight to them. On a percentage scale of one to a hundred percent, how sad are you? *I feel 60 percent sad, 20 percent frustrated and 20 percent tired.* In your automatic thought record you would make notes: On this day in this situation, you feel this way, this much. That's valid!

Next, examine the circumstances or reasons around how you feel. What additional context can you provide to help you understand your feelings? What may be some alternative thoughts? *Well, it's been a rough week. I've had more pain than usual, I didn't sleep well. I'm fatigued.*

What might be an alternative positive or balanced thought? *It's reasonable if I've had a week of pain not to sleep well. Which is why I'm tired... And I'm out of my favorite coffee creamer.*

You could feel stuck because you don't have the resources you need to put yourself into your best position. It's reasonable to feel emotions, even if they're strong. Own it and validate that. Automatic negative thoughts can trick us into thinking "This is the way it is." Then you process it and experience this event as a permanent state. An alternative balanced thought says, "This is not permanent and maybe there's an underlying reason for how I feel." As you go through these questions, validate what you feel — weigh it. Think like an observer and bring in all the context, then you can reach a more balanced thought.

Self-awareness is knowing that in the absence of information, in the absence of examination, narratives form. We fill in the gap. Your more balanced thought might be: *Yeah, tough morning. Not as resourced as I usually am. A tough morning doesn't mean I have a tough life. Or that the day is ruined. Or that the pain won't be reduced.*

You might remember that you haven't yet stretched or exercised. By forcing yourself to observe your thoughts, and challenging the negative narrative, you can get unstuck. The longer you're stuck, the more you develop a narrative around it. And the more likely it is to become truth — until it finally is challenged. You'll find an automatic thought record chart in the appendix on page 229.

Belief or Truth

I'm blessed to be in a circle of women who think the world of each other. It's the way female friendships should be. They are so supportive, and when they throw ideas out, they're more than willing to follow through on them. We stand by each other in the celebrations and the sorrows. They're a huge support and quick to call you out on stuff that isn't for your best.

Over the course of dinner with a new friend, I was surprised by the question she asked.

"Are you applying your wisdom to yourself?"

I love when someone sees past whatever I did

and can challenge me. People rarely do. This is a form of receiving input and that is love to me.

After my dinner with my new friend, I went through my own automatic thought record. I've been frustrated with several things going on, tired from keeping up with my granddaughter, and weary with pain. My automatic thoughts go to, "I get to make it to this age, I didn't think I was going to live this long. I'm happily married and get to live this great life. I have a beautiful granddaughter. And this is how you're going to finish out with me, Lord? In pain? Maybe in a wheelchair in a couple of years?"

Like all of us, I sometimes let my thoughts take me straight to some of my greatest fears and worst possible circumstances. I've been guilty of falling into a negative loop and seeing my story play out like a movie and how it affects the people I love. Eventually, I recognize the narrative and notice that I'd jumped to a conclusion that hasn't happened — and that likely may never happen.

The conversation with my friend challenged me regarding where I live mentally. Interestingly, I constantly remind clients of that very thing: *This is the day you have.* We don't live in tomorrow; we don't live in yesterday. Yesterday is gone, but you can bring all of yesterday's experiences to today. I can choose to use that knowledge to make the next step better.

Pain prevents me from doing some of the things I want to do. In my mind, I'm constantly working out the logistics about what I can and can't do based on my self-awareness and personally known limitations. I struggle from time to time when I see loved ones enjoying their level of physical ability. I sometimes ache for the things I was once able to do.

During my thought examination process, I validate my fears. They're real to me and not completely baseless. My mobility is hindered, but I do not live in the narrative that I imagined. I have the opportunity to create a perspective that's more open and that may create other solutions. I don't yet know because I don't live there yet, and maybe I never will. I live in today. If I'm so afraid of what's going to happen tomorrow, I miss the opportunities of today.

Was I in pain at my dinner with my new friend? Yes, so much so that I almost canceled because I didn't want to show up on a cane, with a lady I didn't know that well. If I'm stuck and worrying over showing up "like that," I don't show up and have that dinner.

My more balanced thought was, "Girl, take

some Advil! It's cold enough for you to wear those leather jeans you really like. Put on sneakers. Yes, she's probably going to have on pumps and something really elegant, because that's the job she does. That's what she's coming from today. But that isn't where you're coming from. Just go!"

I did, and she was delightful!

I'm so glad I didn't let a pity party keep me from a delightful and enlightening experience. Had I sat home, I would have ordered food that wasn't ideal and felt bad about the whole thing. I would have missed something truly wonderful. Thank you, Lord, for allowing me to go and live in the moment. We had fun. God blessed the evening, and He blessed my morning the next day! Because I took the time to examine what was going on internally, process them, and move through.

This illustrates how easily we can derail ourselves and how important it is to catch it. Not to beat ourselves up, but to say here's where I am, here's how I got off track, and now I'm going to get myself back on. If you don't catch it right away, it's okay! You'll get better at seeing it as you practice self-awareness and this expanded level of self-care. You'll get back on track as you're able — in your way. Your soul will thank you.

Finishing Strong

Often people are reticent to talk about things from their hurtful past because they don't want to relive it. The thing that hurt you back there isn't here, but you are here. You lived through it and survived it already. You live here now. You're not living through that again. To examine it isn't to relive it.

The final point I want people to understand about moving onward is that nothing is linear. You might have said, "I thought I was done with this! And here it shows up again." We're talking about breaking lifelong patterns. Things that were part of your personality construct, things that were part of your family of origin, or childhood trauma; you can't undo those things. They're real. At this point you'll have a different perspective; they're part of how you move about in life. When you look back, you don't reexperience them. Or when you feel like you're doing a loop of some sort, you're doing it from a place of experience, not reliving.

Addiction medicine offers us a template. The current philosophy on the addiction process is that recovery is cyclical, and relapse is a part of it. You're in recovery and have a fall. Maybe it's at a different place in your loop, or that the loop is smaller. Each time, you gather experience or knowledge about yourself or your triggers. Eventually you get out of the loop. You have another layer of the onion peeled.

Addiction comes from avoidance, so if you're in recovery, you must deal with the things you've avoided. That hurts! You avoided them for a reason. Healing is hard. At some point you have enough of a lift to step out of the circle. You look at the past with learning, success, and opportunity for the creation of a new narrative. You can reframe how you are in this process and move to the next thing. Life will bring you something else, but it may not be that. There might be a lot you learned about yourself that you can take into the next situation. Although healing is painful, it's a process only you can undertake for yourself.

If you got stabbed, you were cut with a knife. If you had surgery, you are still cut with a knife. Stabbing is unto wounding. Surgery is unto healing. It still hurts. It's still a cut, you still bled, you'll need to get stitches and take care of the wound and any infection. All the things you need to heal from a stab wound, you need to heal from a surgical wound.

What's the direction you're taking? What story

are you telling yourself through your healing process? It hurts to stay sick. It hurts to get well. One takes from your life, but the other brings life.

When I began writing this book, I was in a tough season and to some extent, it's still tough. I've endured some deeply felt disappointments, which are still disappointing, but they don't overtake me. I'm in a different place mentally than when I began writing. I've been able to release what is not mine to do. If we don't examine our experiences and learn about ourselves, we'll continue repeating those negative patterns.

It is my hope that this book will convey that your life is yours to live, granted and purposed by the Creator. You choose how to live it. With access to resources, gifts, and talents, you can turn many of your negative experiences into pivotal moments that will bring you a greater self-awareness. And in doing so your self-care will become your superpower. Your soul will be nourished.

For Your Consideration

1. Where have you not processed a significant hurt and chose to move on rather than move through?
2. When you examine your thoughts, is the story negative or positive?
3. What narrative are you currently believing that has not yet happened? What phrase can you create to snap yourself back?

Appendix

AUTOMATIC THOUGHT RECORD
7 COLUMN PROCESSING GRID

SITUATION/ CIRCUMSTANCE	EMOTIONS/ FEELINGS (RATE 0-10)	UNHELPFUL/ DISTURBING THOUGHTS AND IMAGES	EVIDENCE THAT SUPPORTS THE UNHELPFUL THOUGHT	EVIDENCE THAT DOES NOT SUPPORT THE UNHELPFUL THOUGHT	MORE BALANCED THOUGHTS AND PERSPECTIVES	OUTCOME (RATE 0-10)
The facts: What? Where? When? Who? How?	What emotions/ feelings arose? (Rate the intensity) What sensations did I feel in my body? Describe them.	What thoughts, memories or images went through your mind?	What are the facts? What do I know to be true?	What is not true? Could it be opinion over fact?	STOP AND TAKE A BREATH... Am I considering all of the context? Is there another way to see this? Is there a bigger picture? Am I extending grace to myself?	Is there a change in the intensity of my emotions/ feelings? Did I discover anything helpful in processing these types of emotions and feelings?

Davia Williams-Stevenson 2024, adapted from Padesky 1995. Permission to use for therapy purposes.

Appendix

ABOUT THE AUTHOR

Davia Williams Stevenson is a licensed clinical counselor, life coach, speaker, entrepreneur, podcaster, and author. She has spent over fourteen years guiding couples, families, and individuals towards mental and relational health.

Davia holds a Bachelor of Arts in Psychology from the University of Oklahoma and a Masters in Clinical Counseling from Ashland Theological Seminary. She's a member of the American Counseling Association, the Ohio Counseling Association, and The Association for Spiritual, Ethical and Religious Values in Counseling.

She currently lives in central Ohio with her husband and family. She can be found on Facebook, Instagram, YouTube and DaviaStevenson.com.

Made in the USA
Middletown, DE
18 October 2024